THE EIGHTH MOON

THE
EIGHTH
MOON

A Memoir of
Belonging and Rebellion

JENNIFER KABAT

MILKWEED EDITIONS

Published 2024 by Milkweed Editions
Printed in the United States of America
Cover design by Mary Austin Speaker
Cover art: "Untitled, 2021," by Joan Nelson, courtesy of the artist and
Adams and Ollman; photography by Area Array
Author photo by CJ Harvey
24 25 26 27 28   5 4 3 2 1
First Edition

Library of Congress Cataloging-in-Publication Data

Names: Kabat, Jennifer, 1968- author.
Title: The eighth moon / Jennifer Kabat.
Description: First edition. | Minneapolis, Minnesota : Milkweed Editions,
2024. | Includes bibliographic references. | Summary: "In a braided
chronology, this debut memoir synchronizes the story of a move to rural
Upstate New York with the Anti-Rent War of the nineteenth century"--
Provided by publisher.
Identifiers: LCCN 2023029968 | ISBN 9781639550685 (paperback) | ISBN
9781639550692 (ebook)
Subjects: LCSH: Kabat, Jennifer, 1968- | Margaretville (N.Y.)--Biography. |
Country life--New York--Margaretville. | Women authors,
American--Biography. | Women socialists--United States--Biography. |
Antirent War, N.Y., 1839-1846. | Socialism--New York (State)--History. |
Catskill Mountains Region (N.Y.)--History.
Classification: LCC F127.D3 K33 2024 | DDC 974.7/36092
[B]--dc23/eng/20231018
LC record available at https://lccn.loc.gov/2023029968

Milkweed Editions is committed to ecological stewardship. We strive to
align our book production practices with this principle, and to reduce
the impact of our operations in the environment. We are a member of the
Green Press Initiative, a nonprofit coalition of publishers, manufactur-
ers, and authors working to protect the world's endangered forests and
conserve natural resources. *The Eighth Moon* was printed on acid-free
30% postconsumer-waste paper by Versa Press.

For my parents, and for David, always

"To articulate what is past does not mean to recognize 'how it really was.' It means to take control of a memory, as it flashes in a moment of danger."

—WALTER BENJAMIN,
Theses on the Philosophy of History

THE EIGHTH MOON

Part I

GENTIAN

Chapter 1

1845. THE SKY IS BLUE, yet all is brown. I can taste it. Dried straw and hay and dirt, dust, sweat, and mud—because even in a drought, and it is a drought, one that's been called biblical—a farmyard has muck and manure. I picture the scene from overhead: chaos; a silvered steel of violence, blood, beer, whiskey, and mutton. High, skidding clouds skip with excitement, eager to see what unfolds below. They cheer on the scene where men in dresses march. The men look like sepiaed clowns.

Nearby, two officials in black, sheriff and lawyer, confer in the dooryard. They are named Moore and Wright, as if to say actually, truly, their names are Less and Wrong. They are here to auction off the farmer's livestock. They haggle and talk, no need for whispers because the law is on their side, because they are the law, and before them everyone—bystanders and clowns, those men in drag—all are breaking the law, a new regulation banning disguises enacted eight months previous. Wright digs out his pocket watch.

The men in dresses parade four abreast from house to barn and back again. Their gowns— or is it nightshirts; they are loose and baggy—swirl with rusted paisleys and black checks, even red flannel, though it is sweltering. The dresses cover the men's clothes, their wool pants and shirts. Pantaloons dangle low to conceal even the men's boots, anything that might identify the wearer. All of the

3

marchers sport masks made of leather, a gash of red fabric stitched on for mouths. Gaping holes are left for eyes, and each mask is tied tightly with twine at the neck. No one can it rip it off to expose the person underneath.

———

Moore and Wright (Less and Wrong), confer about where the posse is, when the undersheriff and his constable, who are brothers-in-law, will arrive with reinforcements. Wright, the lawyer, voice peevish and pinched, demands to know. Moore must, he says, be aware of his subordinates' whereabouts.

Wright wears a long coat with nipped waist that is the fashion of the time, one that requires a corset, one that now in this heat is too tight, and his breath is choked. His top hat reaches for the heavens to assert the height of his authority. It is not the sort of hat that is practical for sun or labor, not this sort of morning. He carries a cane with a shiny silver top and has been wondering if it might protect him, if the silver could be a weapon against the masked men. He takes a rough guess of their numbers—150, 200, more? He demands again to know of the posse. Or should we make these onlookers our agents? The law gives them that power too.

In the bars, the corral, the cows low. They too are brown. Into this unceasing amber of heat and drought, an old gaunt man emerges from the house. His wife—even older and gaunter, skinnier and sallow, she in her seventies—remains inside, hidden. He steps forth but cannot manage to move beyond the stoop. His name is Moses Earle. The barn and man and house are all faded. The weathered boards are the color of an old-man's beard, and the barn is so small we'd call it a shed. It lists to the side like a sigh.

Earle wears his best clothes to meet this day with honor.

Wright and Moore, Wrong and Less, are to sell his "property," six cows and eight pigs, assessed at $131 to cover $64 of
rent in arrears, more than twice what he owes. The amount
is meant to be punitive. The lawyer is the agent for a woman,
Charlotte Delancey Verplanck, whose family owns hundreds
of thousands of acres in these Catskill Mountains. She con-
trols nearly the farmer's entire township of Andes, New York,
and she has never once been to the town, not even to visit.
Usually Earle travels the 150 miles to New York City to pay
the rent, but no longer. He stands in solidarity with his neighbors, tenant farmers who have decided to go on rent strike.
They are all poor and broke, farming poor and broken land in
debt peonage where they will have to pay rent into perpetuity. The strike has been going on for a year now with battles,
blood, and jail for the protesters.

—

The men in dresses turn with a flourish, in a mockery
of military maneuvers. None have fought in a war, but
their fathers and uncles and grandfathers have, in the
Revolutionary War and the War of 1812. They march and
sing and brandish arms. They carry rifles, pistols, fowling
pieces, weapons that, if they do not own, neighbors and
allies have slipped them. Others bear axes and swords and
knives with foot-long blades like something a pirate would
use to flay a man. The marchers taunt in a sing-song, making up lyrics as they go:

> *Oh dear what can the matter be*
> *Dear dear what can the matter be*
> *What shall I do with my tenants*
> *How shall I get my illegal rents*

Under the masks, sweat drips into the eyes, stinging. Still the men leer. A cheer rises; someone with horsehair braids and red trim trailing his mask yells, "Moore will not be able to deliver your filthy money."

One of the marchers calls out a verse:

The Andes boys are playing the dickens
The violence sweeping around me now thickens
With killing off rent and landlords some of us quicken

Someone interrupts, "Or, killing off the sheriff."

Oh dear what can the matter be.

Drunken laughter crashes on the hills. The dresses sway together like swells of grass, and men pick up with the refrain. The one who'd sung the verse warbles in a falsetto:

My tenants once came to my office aflocking
Some without shoes or a coat or their stockings
You'd think it would be upsetting and shocking
But now I will get no more rent

As they march, more men in dresses materialize from the hills and woods and bushes, as if the men are mist and plants themselves.

———

Compared to his neighbors, Moses Earle is wealthy. He owns half his farm and still he is poor. It is not worth the money to paint the house or barn when the premises are not yours, not really. When your only property is your livestock that the landlord can seize without even going to court, what is the point of painting? Of care, of improving? Of doing any extra labor? It is now years into a recession and the drought has made wheat scarce. Zoom in on the stoop, and this old man, he swallows. Beneath his beard his cheek throbs.

The legions of men campaigning in the road break off. A cordon of forty spreads out in a line from house to barn, shoulder to shoulder. In the masks they hold their breath against the unceasing swelter and its smell, lest the leather push the stench back on you. A few of the men have plucked clover to hold between their teeth.

Up and down the line, a pail is passed, perhaps with beer or something stronger. Moore and Wright have stopped at the tavern on their way to Earle's this morning. Less and Wrong, clowns and bystanders, all are tight—drunk even the Old-School Baptists.

—

A young woman darts out and guides the gaunt farmer inside. "Earle, come. You know right is right."

Zoom in on the two men in black. The lawyer accuses the sheriff of failing again to hold an auction. Every sale Moore has presided over for months has been interrupted by the men in dresses and masks. Wright, the lawyer, taunts, "Did you plan such on purpose, Moore?"

Here the sheriff glances away. He steps on a weed, a lowly plantain. In the drought even the weeds with deep taproots are stunted. The small scraggly plant hugs the ground and bears a promise to heal wounds, a portent of what will come. No one sees it, and why would you—unless you are hungry, unless you know you can cook it for a bitter meal.

Look past the two men, their feet in the dirt by the barn, its unstained boards. Nailed to the building's side is a sale notice. Close in on the metal nails piercing paper. Two florid Ds are printed with curlicues: Distrain & Distress. Above them in even bigger letters DISTRESS SALE. Just whose distress is open for interpretation. The law points to its being the landlord's, but it is all around us in the men in dresses and their hunger. Charlotte Verplanck's name is listed as the auction's beneficiary, Wright as her representative. The sale is to take place at 1 p.m. It has been postponed a week already, for fear of violence.

The sheriff turns to face the crowd gathering along the stone wall. He wonders if the auction can happen at all. So many of the sales have gone wrong for him. Beneath his boot, the plantain is pulverized; what juice was in its leaves congeals in the dust. It is just gone noon on August 7, and it is a good day for haying.

———

I picture the early morning that day, mist rising from the river below. Boys, men, and teenagers cross the fields carrying bundles wrapped in pillowcases that conceal their disguises. They hide in the trees and bushes. Some people report Scottish being spoken. I am sure it is just English with an accent, but maybe it is Gaelic. Others overhear songs of enlisting from the old country.

By a spring, food is laid out—mutton and beef and pork, eight loaves of bread, and butter in a pail spread across a tablecloth. In their paisley and calico, the men chew and joke about what they'll do when the man Steele appears. The undersheriff is their sworn enemy. He has beaten them and tortured their wives, taken to arresting anyone he can, anyone he suspects. The law gives him liberal powers.

Someone with a mouth full of bread says, "We won't shoot the animals but the bidders."

———

The men are here because the property is to be auctioned off. For a tenant farmer, his property is not land or anything in his home but his livestock, the animals. They hold the value.

———

It is 1845 but could be 1877 or 1893 or 1915, 1932 or 1974, 1983, 2008 or 2009, all the years hard luck comes. Laws and banks and money circle round.

———

The sheriff needs to drive the cattle from the lower pasture up the hill for the sale and asks someone to help.

"No, I wouldn't like to do that," the man replies. Technically, legally, he is obliged to assist. The antimask law passed in January requires it. He tries to hide his hands behind his back as if that alone could protect him. "Can you ask some other one?"

Sheriff, voice dipping as with kindness: "There will be no harm. They won't abuse you."

The man begs him again to find another.

Two volunteers set off with the six cows. A dozen, fifteen, seventeen men move against them. The one in front with his leering mask raises a sword. He holds it to one of the drover's chests. The blade parts the rough linen shirt. He's not intending to hurt him, just scare him a little. A thin line of blood seeps through the fabric. The stain looks like a petal.

In the woods they devour the bread and butter. The town is known for its butter, famous for its sweetness, for the women who churn and skim. Everyone has mostly had to forgo butter, though. They've had to sell all that could be made. Money is scarcer than wheat. They've subsisted on crackers made of bitter dock seeds and cattail's pollen.

Where is the posse, the lawyer demands. "Your men, those brothers, is it; Steele and Edgerton?"

"Brothers-in-law," the sheriff corrects.

The two of them, sheriff and lawyer, talk of relocating the sale to the road to avoid the militants. The sheriff is desperate for any measure that will ensure the auction takes place, and the lawyer, he wants his due; he wants his client's due. The protesters are breaking the law and they must be broken. After so many months of this insurgency, the rebels must be put in their place.

A laborer steps forward. His name is Brisbane. He has a broad Scottish accent, and his hat is squashed down against the beating sun. His brother is one of the men in dresses. Brisbane has lived in this country a handful of years and gives rousing addresses to the protesters about liberty and freedom and how no one owns the land, it belongs to all. Two weeks before, he told the gaunt man of the house not to pay his debt. To do so after so much time and struggle and so many speeches would be hypocrisy. Now he asks the lawyer if he has the right to move the auction.

Lawyer Wright, with his nipped waist: "Do you want to dictate to the sheriff?"

"Nay sir, I do not dictate to you or any man." Brisbane touches his hat and explains that the notice says the auction will be on the premises. Moving the sale into the highway will render it illegal. And, look at the crowds, the bystanders but also the Calico Indians, he calls the men in their disguises.

The sheriff yells, "It is my pleasure to do so." Just what that exact pleasure is, remains unclear, but he must sound resolute before the lawyer. Moore (Less) searches the hoard, knowing that none of them will bid. Or, if they do, it will be only a penny or a dollar to spoil the sale. Or they will keep the bidding going so long into the night the sale will have to be forfeited. He also knows the militants are just as likely to shoot the livestock so it has no value, then they'll take a collection for the farmer to cover the cost of the dead animals. The insurgents call it a tax.

Brisbane again implores them not to move to the road. He worries about the violence that might come; he worries about his younger brother, Robert. He feels responsible for him and thinks of their time in steerage on the crossing to America and the loneliness both felt at first in this new country.

"Is that a threat?" the lawyer says to Brisbane and drives his cane into the dirt.

In the breeze, braids wave behind the masks. Ribbons are woven into horsehair plaits. One disguise has stitched-on eyebrows like old man Earle's. Bushy and made of deer hide, the fur knits in a quizzical expression. A pendant is affixed to the temple. The medal looks military, like a badge of authority, but is nothing more than Poseidon and a couple of mermaids. It was just the only shiny brass thing to hand.

Another group appears from the woods. Their leader,

in a red dress and red cloth mask, calls out for the chief of Andes, whom he calls Pompey. The man in scarlet asks to be made commander. A show is made of the transfer of power. Pompey hands him a silver sword and nods, and this man Bluebeard, he is named, is now in charge. Bluebeard in his scarlet costume holds the sword to the lawyer's breast.

The lawyer's knuckles go white as he grips his cane. In the distance a horn is blown.

Bluebeard says to step back twenty feet.

Someone yells, "We've got the chaps we want." The call rises from down the road, repeated and repeated. "They are here."

In the muddy farmyard, the lawyer Wright/Wrong says, "I am here to protect property."

Two men on gray steeds ride up. Earth and dust billow in their wake.

The man in scarlet: "You have no property, and if you bid on the property, we will shoot you."

Lawyer: "I won't move an inch for you or any of your tribe. You leave me alone or I'll make you leave me alone." He touches his pocket where his pistol is. He doesn't take it out. He doesn't need to.

The Bluebeard in his red dress pulls out his gun. "If you don't take away, I'll put a hole in you."

"I know you, Scudder." The lawyer uses Bluebeard's given name, or the name he suspects.

Bluebeard, "You can't swear to it."

———

The men arriving on horseback are Steele and Edgerton, undersheriff and constable. Steele has a toothpick in his mouth and red hair, and they stopped at a tavern on the way, too.

They ride down the line. The protesters call out: "You'll chew something harder." Meaning a bullet and not the toothpick. "We'll make your red hair redder." Another: "You bid, you will go down feet foremost in a wagon." In other words: dead.

The lawmen and lawyer meet. Steele and his constable were to bring a posse, but there is no posse, no one to back them up. They ride to the barn to read the sale notice and make to leave, whether out of fear or because they are out-numbered or to muster support or for a more opportune moment is unclear. The costumed men force them back.

Bluebeard calls out for the bystanders to move and make way. He and his men head to the pasture to surround the cattle.

The men on steeds circle the lot, and the sheriff and Wright try to enter. The clowns lock arms to keep them out, and the lawyer shoves in with his cane. Someone knocks off his silk hat. "Touch me again and I'll shoot you," he says. He bends for it and brushes it off. With that, the top hat on the ground, the kneeling, the dusting and taunt-ing, his frail failure in this moment, his rage rises. It has a taste, a smell: his breakfast that morning and sawdust in the tavern, a wink in the eye of the man who served them.

The gaunt old man appears again at his door. He calls out that he's paid rent enough, he reckons. But, this must end. He has a pocketbook in hand, and the young woman in an apron is suddenly next to him. She grabs his arm and the wallet. He yells her name, Parthenia, or tries to. His voice only croaks. He has said he was okay with the hogs being killed but not the cattle—and not people, not this, not violence. She hides the money in her dress and drags him back in by the hand. "You cannot undo what is done."

More of the clowns, the costumed men circle the corral. They flood in from the road and forest, standing two, three deep at the bars. Scudder, this Bluebeard in his red dress, commands, "Shoot the horses."

Steele: "Shoot my horse and I shoot you." Together the two men, constable and undersheriff, make to jump the fence side by side. They spur their horses and canter together and leap the wall. The constable is ahead by a nose and yells out to keep the peace three times. "I command—" Chaos, dirt, mud in the yard, everything everyone, happens at once—the swirling dresses, weapons raised, horses whinnying, and the cattle braying in distress.

———

But the officers' guns are out, and the constable leads. It is unclear who fires first. Gunpowder is acrid and burns in the nose.

The two men gallop.

Scudder yells again to shoot the horses.

Edgerton shouts, "I command the peace. All citizens are to assist in the peace."

Steele: "I dare you to shoot my horse."

Edgerton: "First man stops me driving the cattle for the sale I will shoot, shoot him dead."

There is a cry, "Shoot or drop horses."

The men leap together.

They are in the air.

Shots are fired.

Balls sing. Lead flies. Two flashes; six, eight guns are fired. Their pistols are out. They are over the fence. Steele's horse turns his head toward the wall. Steele is in the act of firing, his hand raised.

Edgerton's horse wheels and falls. Steele's horse rises. Edgerton pushes himself up and stumbles toward the men, his weapon in the air. Steele lifts his pistol. Steele rides in a circle around the men in dresses making to fire. He rides at them directly. His pistol is up. He grabs his horse's mane. The bullet comes for his mount. The animal canters to the left. Steele leans forward. A ball arrives for him, for his bowels. His coat flaps fly up. The horse stumbles three steps forward. He and the horse collapse together.

People run. They scatter for the road and hill. A few rush toward the fallen man. Edgerton sprints toward Steele and yells, "You murderers."

Chapter 2

2005. I KNOW NONE OF these events when I move a few miles away to the next town over, Middletown and its village of Margaretville. I cycle past green fields and a lone blue historical marker: "ONE MILE TO SCENE OF TRAGEDY WHERE UNDERSHERIFF OSMAN M. STEELE WAS SLAIN BY ANTI-RENTERS, AUGUST 7, 1845." The State Education Department erected it in 1932, and later I come to think of a link between the years, between the Depression and 1932 and 1845, but that will be a decade more in a future tense.

I see that scene like a movie. Watch the actors strip out of costumes and pull off the dresses and pantaloons. Underneath, they wear jeans, running shoes, and hiking boots. Someone calls out about bug spray. "Want the kind that kills ticks or the hippy stuff?" Others amble to the craft service table, but the sky is still that cerulean that feels like an ache because it goes on forever.

At first for me everything here is simply pastoral. Endlessly peaceful: fields and forests and stone walls snaking up to oblivion.

—

We come because I am sick. I have chronic fatigue. Impossible exhaustion. In London where my husband and I lived, I toured the offices of environmental doctors, in their name a promise to treat something so global it's everywhere all the time, as if my sickness is everything. And, for me it was, it was the city and the air itself. My first week living in the UK, I broke out in a rash. It was from washing powder but could seem to be the move itself.

I went there to live with my husband. He, David, became my husband so we could be in the same country and same city. For most people at our stage in a relationship, that would be dating. But, I was in New York and he a seven-hour flight away, a distance too far and too expensive to transcend. The answer: marriage. Neither of us believed in it. Matrimony is a product of capitalism and Christianity, and that we could promise to have and hold and some other vows that would bind us legally together just to live in the same city seemed wrong. Gay marriage wasn't legal, and until all could marry, our doing so also seemed wrong. Not to mention the fact that marrying could be seen as an easy immigration dodge for me, a white woman. Nonetheless, I was now a year out of an MFA and three years into this marriage and had visited multiple doctors all to try to cure what we called "my health." The word itself was a stone, a weight to carry around.

A headache would bloom or my throat would swell, my lips come up in blisters—on the inside, on the tender side. Or I'd come down with a flu, though it was not the flu, not something that anyone could detect or diagnose as a virus, and I'd be in bed for three days. Feeling better, I'd walk too far or ride a bike or wander past someone smoking or smell someone smoking some 200 yards away, or breathe in bus exhaust or something I couldn't even detect or name, and my lower back would ache and my bones would get sore, my hands sore, then my throat and sinuses sore, and this flu/not-flu would return and I would return to bed. My life whittled down to a fine point, to the fine point of my bedroom and desk, of being stuck at home and sick in Britain, a new country I barely knew.

I had tests, changed my diet, cut this, restricted that, added in expensive vitamins and something called chelation therapy delivered through an IV. There was meditation and I followed regulations, different ones from each doctor—a litany of regimens including giving myself shots in the thigh every other day. None of it worked, or not enough.

———

Doctor's office. Tuesday afternoon: oatmeal, gray, and beige—colors of no color. This in a dull outer-London suburb already two trains from my own outer suburb. I remember now a bland carpet, but it couldn't have been carpeting, just drab. These doctors don't have rugs or carpets. One of the first things I learned is that such soft furnishings could make us sick. I was also part of an "us" now, a group of sick people. The doctor flicks at my file, my life, it felt like.

Move, he said. You cannot stay in London. Manila folders sit in stacks on his desk. More drab, bland shades. Early on he'd commanded: never paint, no new cars, VOCs could . . . His voice had droned on. Stop shopping. No new clothes. He'd said something about their having formaldehyde.

This Tuesday I was sure from the sound of his voice he'd had this conversation countless times.

How long before we can come back? My voice arced up. Everything in David's and my lives has been aimed at cities. We'd both moved to our own cities as soon as we were eighteen.

If I follow protocols, this doctor says, six months, a year, two. Well, three.

So, exile.

———

That winter: David and I stand on Regent Street. An argument. We have to leave your city, I said. The "you" was underlined with accusation. The city belonged to him whenever things went wrong. He reached for my shoulder. There was the soft burr of his voice, lamplight phosphorescing in the damp December night. Humid air held more pollution, we'd learned. A sinus headache bored into my brain, the colors red and blaring. On the street, with the impossible exhaustion of mine, he hailed a cab.

Inside, I angled away from him, and there is so much in this moment that reveals David, this man gentle, kind and generous, who is willing to leave his city for the unknown, for my health. I stared at the window, spoke to the glass. My breath fogged it. I laid down an ultimatum. This time next year we must be gone. He didn't argue. I wanted him to fight back. My voice rose. We must go. He touched my knee. The driver eyed me in the rearview mirror, and we could not afford this cab to our house in the outer suburb, and yet. This man married me only so we could date, and we were both held hostage to my being sick.

I was also homesick, but that wasn't the problem. I was allergic to London, which could be a metaphor but is, in fact, perfume, car exhaust, diesel fumes, cigarette smoke, and the formaldehyde fire retardant used in clothes. London itself is a bowl that collects pollution, and these pollutants settle in the city.

David's name is Rainbird. Rain+bird is how I sound it out for people so they understand. Americans will ask if he is Native American, and I say, No, bird names come from the east of England. Or that it is French, a broken and corrupted version of "fox," *reynard*. I even thought of taking his name because it sounds so romantic, though no one in my family changed names upon marriage, and a friend, the novelist Lynne Tillman, instructed that I could not adopt his no matter how poetic it was. He offered to take mine. Now, we are a couple who have crossed seas and skies to be together. When we married, we had spent no more than twelve days together, the sort of time that sounds like foolishness or a fairytale. Then we leave London for a place that looks like a fairytale, for a house adorned with gingerbread. We move to Margaretville, NY, me and this rain and bird.

First there are lists, spreadsheets. We consider going anywhere we have ever been that is not a city, because to leave all cities, where do you go? Particularly when your existence has been aimed at the urban, at places of burnishing and polishing, where you feel part of the forward march of the future, of art and design, music, clubs, parties and writing, scenes of noise and vibration, where people have to shout as they ask what you are working on, where "work" isn't a job but identity. In those moments I tightened my insides, shellacked my outsides, and felt aglow with possibility.

—

The doctor suggested Greece. We've been to Crete; we consider it. One town has a flight once a week, four hours direct to London. I think the other days of the week are given to military jets. This town has cell service but little internet. Neither of us would be able to work.

Or a desert, the doctor said. Arizona.

On our spreadsheets I calculate the cost of living. If we go to the United States, how will we afford health insurance? I never do get an answer. I call insurance providers whose names promise crosses and shields, anthems and fidelity. Friends in New York give advice, and still we vastly under-estimate the amount. I now too have a pre-existing condition of "my health."

And, David, he has a small design partnership, a two-person firm with his best friend, that has two younger employees. We are all young, and he and his best friend started the partnership the year we marry, in the six months of our long-distance courtship. David and I believe he can be in two places at once, that the internet will allow him to bridge the distances.

One other factor: my elderly parents. My father has a rare blood disorder and is in and out of the hospital. My mother has a cancer that is right now not killing her, but also not cured. I am their late, last child and need to be near enough to get home for the ever-increasing number of emergencies.

—

The final place on the list: the Catskills. It seems vaguely practical. It's a few hours to New York City. David can get to London; I can get to my parents outside Washington, DC, in a seven-hour drive. I also say it's like Vermont, though how could I know? Neither of us has been to the Catskills, and David has never seen the Green Mountain State. I spent my childhood vacations in Vermont, though, two weeks each summer on the side of a mountain at a defunct ski area. By then my sisters had left home, and my parents were often exhausted by me. They would send me outside to pick wildflowers. I'd walk down the dirt road past one switchback and another and scamper down a ravine to skinny dip in a stream called Roaring Brook. Or, I'd hike to the summit and climb onto rusted chairlifts and imagine what it would be like to soar down a mountain in snow. None of this do I explain to David, not the way loneliness felt nor how it was held in the flowers I dried, whose names I recorded in books, lists that I held as totems of that time. But he says okay.

—

There is also all we don't know about Margaretville: the mountains, the ridges, the reservoirs, the streams and floods, the spring that arrives at the end of May, frost in August, snow in October. Or, that the land here is of two places. Most of it belongs to New York City, though the city is more than a hundred miles away. This is the city's watershed, and the municipality is the largest landowner across 1600 square miles in a bid to protect its water, its six reservoirs. It even has a police force to guard the water.

We also know little of the hardship, that this is the northernmost part of Appalachia, according to the federal government's official designation. Or, the average earnings hovering near the poverty line. Or, that the village we move to is named for a woman, Margaret Lewis Livingston, whose family is related to the Verplancks, and that Livingstons and Verplancks once owned all this land, a feudal kingdom where tenants were bound to the land in perpetuity.

———

The fairytale house sits on the corner of Walnut and Orchard Streets where neither walnuts nor orchards grow. The neighbors soon will plant an apple tree whose bounty will be free to all. These neighbors are a gay couple whom we come to call the godfathers, because they get together the year we are born, and one of them, we discover, is a distant cousin of mine, a Kabatchnik. His family hails too from the shtetels of Vilnius.

This house is in a row of stately Victorians. The fronts are wrapped with porches. Gables grab for the sky. Ours is called a Queen Anne Victorian, as if being named for two queens makes the place doubly regal. It even has a turret. Inside is ornate woodwork—any possible surface that can be tooled, carved, inlaid, or ornamented is—the moldings, the floors, the railings, the newel posts and staircases, the hall closet and linen cupboards, even. Above every door, the lintels are shaped in three peaks like a crown, and intricate carved wooden beads suggesting an abacus hang over the

French doors between the two living rooms. Things here also come in twos: two staircases and these living rooms. One of them David dubs the parlor. Too fancy for daily use, we never furnish it beyond a couple chairs.

This queenly home gives us space beyond our imaginations. There is a room for every and any activity: work, writing, meditating (if we do it) or yoga (if we practice it) as well as guests. All the friends I've left in New York City can visit—together—it seems. Behind the house a brook called Bull Run babbles. The turret, though, is a folly. Form does not follow function. Outside, it promises turret-ness, climbing to a pointed spire and topped with a ball. Inside it is a just bulging curve where the turret should be, as if the room is distended, angling out with ambitions to escape.

—

October: I do the closing by myself. David is back in London. The air is crisp, and the night will freeze, and I stand before this home with all of its doubles and rooms, so many I can't figure out where to settle or land. How do I write the emotions of being alone for something so big?

Flowers, he sends flowers. They are beautiful and not nearly enough: tea pinks and pale greens spilling from an elegant vintage vase the florist picked out. The florist too is a transplant, so are our realtor and lawyer and the couple from whom we buy the house. Like the godfathers, all of them are gay, and we are heartened to move to a rural town where stickers with rainbow flags appear in windows, as if a decal can dispel our worries about what life might be like here.

—

I think now about beginnings, all of the places this story starts, doctors' offices and bland carpet, marriage—but my opening is here at a desk surrounded by note cards and index cards with headlines taped to a wall alongside quotes from writers I love. There's Elizabeth Hardwick's nascent beginning, her false start for her autobiographical novel *Sleepless Nights*. She was a critic and essayist, one of the cofounders of the *New York Review*. She writes often of other writers and their lives. Her circle of friendships seems synonymous with the city and its intellectual mores at midcentury. The group is tight and cliquish, and I picture her regal, arch: scotch, high heels, cigarettes . . . In the novel, time is dimensional and all at once. She draws from pieces of her criticism in it too, including entire passages from her essays. It's all first-person, present-tense—and past, the times swelling together, as if this is her view of how to write a novel at middle age.

Right now, in the bit I'm hanging on the wall, her project is not a novel yet, but still just an essay in the *New York Review* in the early seventies. She writes of Goethe—the possibilities of beginning, like a threshold as a place to pause. Then she talks about another writer, an unnamed novelist, who "cannot accept a linear motivation as a proper way to write." Instead, it is replaced by "chaos."

—

That day I walk to the end of the block where the road forks. It hews to the stream Bull Run. I follow a shaded lane, also named for this stream, up and up and up for miles it seems, the distance more a factor of my feeling so alone than a measure of how far I've traveled. It's barely a mile, I'll learn. Overhead a tight bower of hemlocks hides the light.

I hear a waterfall and stumble down a bank so steep the soil skids from under my feet. I grab onto a sapling, and a flash of fear courses through me. I am invisible to any passing cars, though no traffic passes. Posted signs are nailed into the hemlocks. I am trespassing and terrified someone might catch me. I listen for any sound. The falls roar. They beckon to a hidden pool. Rocks line the sides as if walls once guarded this spot, and I have happened onto something private and hidden. Above, a channel has been carved into the boulders along the stream. Accident of floods or geology or someone's impossible labor, I have no idea.

Back on the road, a clearing opens to a high valley with a little farmhouse. The barn door is emblazoned in fading paint: SURGE MILKER. Asters bloom in florescent shades of pink and purple next to the last of the goldenrod. A dead-end sign is planted beyond the farm, as if to say go no further.

Standing here in the shiver of aloneness on the road high above the village, I have a shimmering sense of discovery. The place feels like a John Denver song, the one of country roads that promise home—or at least a sense of it: belonging. There is always longing in belonging, though. Plus, this blue, blue sky and a view across to Pakatakan, the mountain that stands over the village. What I don't yet know is that beyond a dead-end sign, a road can continue a mile or more before petering out in a field or someone's driveway or at a gate.

—

This land, that is the start: the waterfall, the posted sign, the farmhouse and the SURGE MILKER—even the battle in the corral—all the things of this very place, farmland turning back to forest. And the million-and-some acres owned by New York City as well. All the water in Brooklyn, Bronx, Queens, and Manhattan has its origins in these mountains, in that stream and its rapids, and in a reservoir nearby called the Pepacton. Right now, though, Margaretville is just a quaint name that people will joke about, "Margaritaville." Later someone asks, "Are you wasting your days away again there?"

The mountain, Pakatakan, is part of the Appalachians, the rubble of the continent's oldest peaks, the ancient Acadian range formed 400 million years ago and once the size of Everest. Now these hills are three and four thousand feet at best. Pakatakan is Munsee Lenape land, land that was sold by a sachem named Cacawalemin. Hendrick Hekan is the Dutch name he took, and the word "sold" brings up many questions: the dates, the money, the records . . . In those records, testimony from white men attests to the fact that Hekan raised apples and produced cider, as if those details were somehow the most important, or else the most familiar to those men. Now the land, his land, is largely protected, part of the Catskill Park and part of the watershed, where the water here belongs to there, to the metropolis where I moved as a teenager on the cusp of adulthood.

Margaretville's Main Street has the dusty feel of a one-horse town, and the village 593 residents. There's a liquor store, kitchen store, thrift store, sandwich shop, grocery store, and two pharmacies, which make it a metropolis compared to other villages nearby. One of the buildings is painted a fussy green and purple with orange detailing. It's called the Bussey Building, as if that rhyme with fussy were intentional and not just the original owners' name. (It was once a dry goods store.) Other buildings have false fronts, facades that extend past the second stories to create a grander impression, more substantial from the street, like our turret and its bulge.

Every day at noon an air raid siren goes off, testing the alarm for the volunteer fire department. The siren calls out first responders, loud enough to reach hills and hollows, but it sounds like a perpetual alert for the Cold War, a call to duck and cover as if that war never ended.

Main Street, Margaretville, N.Y.

———

In her opening to *Sleepless Nights*, Hardwick talks of a building lot. First she says, "muddy tides" of chaos create "a strewn random beach" whose shores border "a house lot always suitable for building." In time, in the high valley near the waterfall we too will find a plot of land, though we cannot afford construction. Instead, we spend summer nights sleeping in a canvas tent that feels permeable to the outside, to the wind and rocks and stone walls and calls of coyotes and owls, the stars and comets, the Milky Way a superhighway across the night sky.

Permeability, that is another beginning, maybe the beginning of all of this. Synesthesia, neurasthenia, the world pressing in on me, time pressing in: lichen and rocks and stars so many billions of light years away crossing the borders of time. I begin to cross time. Only in moving to Margaretville I am first a writer stuck on time and causality: characters, order and plot, things linking up in an orderly direction. And, I support myself by copywriting and some occasional journalism.

Hardwick writes that this writer of hers, the novelist who embraces chaos, doesn't agree with Chekov's law, the one about the gun. If it appears in act one, the rule says, it must go off by the end. Eventually, here guns will be shot.

I begin to write a crime novel, set on this land with the water and its cops. The no-man's land of the watershed is terrain that is here but belongs to New York City. Over the time I live here these holdings swell to almost ten percent of the county, nearly 80,000 acres, all largely empty and unoccupied and hung with posted signs to keep people off. I am obsessed with the land here that belongs to there, that the city even has cops here that belong to there.

I hear rumors of what happens on this city land. Sometimes people dump things they don't want or that are inconvenient. Others grow pot on it. Being sick, I have been driven inside; that is how I originally start to write. Now outside in this world, with the eerie icy winters, the city's swathes of immense, empty space seem threatening. The land is suggestive—or I am suggestive to its dangers. Plus, that police force for water, for trying to control and contain a substance that slips away and streams off. There are also two kids who live on Bull Run. One, the boy, is always silent; the other, a girl, always in her pajamas. I want them to be heroes of a story, so make them the protagonists of this story.

Crime novels, however, demand plot. I fail at it. When I try, my writing is airless and impossible with the *then* and *then* and *then* of orderly time. A friend, a poet, tells me to cut the interstitials. She means all the small elements connecting characters' movements and development. I try to delete the segues and markers of time's passage, the paragraphs that begin, "next week," "this year," "last season," or the sentences that settle a character in space, in a room, on a street, setting the scene around them, but I can't. I try and I try again. Instead I see everything connecting. The writing comes not with the *then* and *then* and *then* of narrative time driven by the hierarchy of information that plot demands, but with the *and* and *and* and *and* of parataxis. Everything is equal all together and all at once.

My gun, it goes off in a different century. It is 1845.

Chapter 3

1949: SEPTEMBER 11, IT IS the second year of the
Cold War and one of the few years of my parents' love.
They marry that day in the backyard of a favorite professor, in Oberlin, Ohio. The handful of people in attendance
include the professor and his wife, like a stand-in for both
my parents' parents, who do not come. There is also my
father's sister and her husband, and her husband's brother.
He is here because he has a car. The three of them have
driven six hours from Pittsburgh. My mom wears a pale-
blue suit and is given a cheap gold ring. A day or so before,
she tells my dad he needs to get her a wedding band. The
way the story comes down it sounds like he doesn't believe
in rings, at least not for weddings, though when I am little
he always brings back ones crafted in silver and turquoise
from his trips in the Southwest.

Other stories I hear: my mom makes the wedding
cake. It's a carrot cake. My parents also do not believe in
marriage; or, not weddings. They are thrilled that David
and I marry in their living room, and I wear a dress bought
on sale and not made for marriage or weddings. Tradition
in my family might be to break traditions. My aunt and uncle, her second husband, marry at a neighbor's when I am
four. The house looks just like ours. My aunt and new uncle stand together in the living room before the plate glass
windows, like David and I come to do. In their wedding

there are dashikis and Afros and a conjoined family. At our ceremony David asks the Unitarian minister not to say God. I don't believe in God, he explains, so why invite him to my wedding? That too pleases my mom.

What else to say about our marriages? My mother's parents don't come to hers because my dad is Jewish. His mother was institutionalized, and he doesn't speak to his father. My aunt and uncle married at the neighbors', I learned recently, because my uncle is Black. It is less than a decade after *Loving v. Virginia* was decided by the Supreme Court, and this is a wedding in the state of Virginia. The rabbi won't marry them in the synagogue.

———

What more about my parents? They both grow up poor. My mom's parents are factory workers in Akron. They lose their home in the Depression. My dad loses more than that. A cross is burned on his lawn when he is little. His father's store goes bankrupt, their home foreclosed, and my dad orphaned, in a sense. His mom has already been hospitalized, and his father, my grandfather, writes his parents that either they take these two kids, meaning my father and my aunt, or else they'll go to the orphanage. They move to Pittsburgh to live with my great-grandparents and sleep in the unheated attic.

My parents meet at Oberlin, two scholarship kids, and they share a dream of a better world—of the collective, socialist and cooperative.

They marry because my father is going to graduate school in public policy—he believes in the public over the private. He asks my mom, this woman named Lois, to move with him. She says they have to be married first.

From what I'm told I think this stand on propriety catches him off guard. Her mother has called her "bohemian," which doesn't mean like a Beat, not yet, but that she wears jeans. This interest in denim dungarees in the late 1940s is unbecoming, apparently. Photos of her show her barefoot in lipstick, jeans, and baggy men's shirts.

After the wedding, my mom and dad, his sister, her husband, and his brother all drive in the brother-in-law's brother's car to Upstate New York. This journey takes hours and hours. No one thought to consult a map or thinks that on those roads, in those cars, in that age before interstates, it might be more than a day's drive. The hours tick, tempers flare and fray, exhaustion sets in. My mom cries because this is not how she pictures the future—crammed into a car and moving to an entirely new state. There are too many people and too little romance. Whatever picture of the future she has isn't materializing, though she's still barely in her twenties and not a traditionalist in any way.

Before my father finishes his degree, he gets a job managing a tiny rural electric co-op. It is in the red and troubled, so troubled that he who comes in third or even fourth for the job when he's interviewed is the only person who will accept it. He does because he sees collectives as his future. And, mine too, it will turn out.

When I'm young, I hear stories of this co-op, of bringing the cat Squeaky to work, of their friendships with farmers and living in a small college town, in a tiny apartment, a cold-water flat they call it, though from the glass walls of our modernist house I don't know what that means. I hear too how they only had beer once a week, as if that explains something to me, a quantifier of class I do not understand. They have a used car on which they owe money, and my mother receives a special dispensation to be the bookkeeper. She has a degree in economics.

I have no photos of the wedding but one of them in front of the co-op with the head lineman Ralph Vaughan. My mom stands in bobby socks in the snow holding the cat. My dad grips a broom. It is now the 1950s. They look like some version of American Gothic but with smiles and, on her, cat-eyed glasses and lipstick. Overhead a sign proclaims ONEIDA-MADISON ELECTRIC CO-OPERATIVE. REA has been painted on both sides of the co-op's name with the "E" as a lightning bolt. The initials stand for Rural Electric Association, a New Deal program. OWNED BY THOSE IT SERVES is stenciled beneath. That phrase is the refrain of my childhood.

———

As a child I have lessons about co-ops and how they are alternatives to capitalism, so too credit unions and land trusts. Everything we buy—orange juice, butter, furniture, and cranberries at Thanksgiving—comes from co-ops, with their shared ownership and profits to the workers, the worker-owners. I hear about co-operatives so much, I think everyone understands this "owned and operated" legend. I don't see them as special or socialism or as having a history tying them to the 1840s and utopias. On vacation in Vermont in the late seventies, my dad takes me to Grange Halls and talks about rural America and collective ownership being farmers' salvation. There are discussions of the importance of nationalizing banks and railways, and when I am ten a black-and-white movie mostly in Norwegian, about immigrant farmers in the Midwest who formed the Nonpartisan League in the nineteen teens. They are socialists in the movie, and in the deep voice he adopts for work, he says that these socialist farmers too are about co-operatives and the people. He uses that phrase, "the people," and explains that his co-operatives developed from this moment. With the way his voice sounds, warm and vibrating in my ribs, I want to be part of "the people" too.

———

This beginning, their beginning in a tiny co-op, is not far from Margaretville, just an hour and a bit on small highways I will begin to travel myself.

Chapter 4

I WRITE THIS STARING OUT at Pakatakan. The mountain's dull-gray rise shoulders over the village, and David is asleep in the turret. Its bulge has become a space that fits a queen-size bed. I sit in the next room, the sunroom, which was once a sleeping porch but is now glassed in. I watch the sky as winter dawn breaks orange and pink. On my desk, I prop two Adrienne Rich books I've had since high school. Just putting them on the desk anoints them—or the desk, or me.

In a poem called "What Is Possible" she writes about "the voices of the ghost-towns." Their lives come in "tiny and vast configurations." Even in solitary silence, these voices and their lives press in. They need understanding, these lives ignored, with the vastness of their existences, of elements that might be seen as marginal or unimportant. I copy the lines and hang them on the wall.

I glance at David through the door. He hugs the pillow, this man on his side with a beard and brown eyes. Generous mouth—a fugue of browns in his face. He is reserved, quiet. He would say this was not exile, our move, but that we find life here, our lives.

His chest rises and falls with his breath, lifting the covers.

ADRIENNE RICH

Scrawled underlining scars the book. A corner is torn from the cover, its paper rough and thick. There's an outline of something like lips I drew when I was seventeen. On the first page a list:

- thank you notes
- read
- service proj

I have no idea what that "proj" was. Underlined in one poem: "social compact." I scribbled next to it "Rousseau / Locke." What did teenaged me think there? Or, what had I been taught to think about these Enlightenment ideals (progress, time, and order)?

Another of Rich's poems has cascading lines about "class privilege" across its pages. The poem is called "Heroines" and will look at these privileges in history. She writes of history as inhabitation, one where we could breathe into the past (or it breathe into us) in a way that is deep and weird, as if we are alive in it.

In high school she and the Victorian art critic John Ruskin were my heroes. Now stuffed in a drawer of this desk are old scraps of paper and notes on the two of them and art history, salvaged from my childhood bedroom. What I didn't say then was how I'd had a crush on him. There was how he championed the working classes and saw the hand labor of the Gothic age as some romantic answer to the Industrial Revolution's deadening work. I thought I was suited to his time. Even at fifteen I was time traveling. I imagined him an intellectual partner, though I knew about his child bride and bad marriage and misogyny.

In London when I was lonely and allergic, where there was so much of my "health" that I had to avoid Central London, I would follow Ruskin's path. He'd also, it turns out, lived in my neighborhood. I joked that our outer suburb was shoved between him and a Clash song, the Brixton Riots and his house. I would visit the Georgian walled garden in the park nearby and then a forest a mile or so away. Alone, that frisson in the air, danger, midday, me, the only one, the only woman, in the woods. I would see him, with his love of nature, walking there too, as if this time were also his time. His time, my time, that teen crush with my ghosts.

It was that same charge as my walk to the clearing up Bull Run, here something thrummed and hummed into me, into the moment. Transported, but I wasn't sure where.

On the cover I colored in the "D" of Wild, the "Λ" in Has. *A Wild Patience Has Taken Me This Far.* And how far Rich herself was taken.

What I liked then and love now is the permeability of history in her poems. In London I'd walk up Ruskin's road, the floury scent of diesel trapped in my throat, and try to figure where he'd lived. He'd set up house next to his parents. Then, there's Adrienne Rich, the past pressing into her present, the two "stitched," she put it, in time. The consciousness of time became her own stream of consciousness: the two run together and become a way to rewrite history. Now on my desk she quotes Jane Addams's letters from her time in Europe as the activist, not yet an activist at all, writes about being lost and "at sea." Searching for "moral purpose."

I see myself walking up Ruskin's road, looking at the faces of blank brick buildings, feeling for some vibration. Only, it's just a truck thundering down the hill, yet here is Addams in Europe too. She is longing not to be in the shadows, longing to be a thinker, longing to matter, longing for "purpose," and this, this is the line that gets me where she says she wants "to live in a really living world." It's the adverb *really* the double *live* and *living* that holds Addams's sheer yearning. And, there I am in London, always sick, always eager, and courting ghosts. Here is Rich too, "marking" Addams's life and using the material conditions of women's lives, to occupy that history and using their quotes to speak for her.

In her writing Rich lives in multiple times. In the collapse of time, in all times.

———

In Margaretville time rips apart. Not far away are the plumose structures where continents split, where Africa broke from what would become North America. "Drift" is the word used for it, but drifting sounds gentle, just slipping away. This fracture happens in a second, at the speed of sound, and what is left in the rocks, though, looks like the impression of a bird's wing in the snow. Nearby is the world's oldest forest, whose trees—ferns, in fact— are now fossils. They are the residue left from floodplains that helped change the air and the soil, "a turning point in earth's history," they've been called.

———

In London I walked sometimes past Buckingham Palace (brick walls, iron bars, guards who looked like a post-card) to hear American accents. Lynne Tillman told me I would miss my language. I did and found myself claustrophobic, all the past pressing in, so much history I couldn't breathe. It felt inescapable. I was trapped by ghosts, and these old buildings massed around me, out-lines of time for which I was not yet ready. I still needed the forward thrum of movement.

———

In the Catskills, I realize that I've moved into a paint-ing. There is Thomas Cole and his waterfalls; Asher Durand and his studies of the land, the vistas moved to the vertical plane with his birches and boulders. The Hudson River School is arrayed across my backyard. I see these paintings on hikes and in the woods and tip my camera on the side to capture boughs, trunks, and boulders like Durand. In one autumn shot, a solar flare pierces the image and the lichen is the only green to be found.

I studied Durand's paintings in high school and college when I thought I would be an art historian. I had dreams of dressing in black and living in a loft and specializing in nineteenth-century American art. I didn't especially like this period, or rather I liked it because it seemed strange and weird, never moving on to Impressionism or any of the revolutions in time and space that European art embraced. Instead the Hudson River School (no school at all, not even a group of paint-ers who felt aligned, but a name coined by a critic) was caught up in nature-as-narrative, and their paintings seemed to fall off the line of art history—or had never made it there in the first place. (I still saw history as a line, those lines about Rousseau and Locke jotted next to Rich's poems.)

In college I would walk to Central Park, to the New York Historical Society, a museum rarely visited and largely empty. I was also anorexic, and the forty-block walk was extra exercise. My younger, early self wanted to disappear, and in the galleries I got to. This slightly psychedelic fledgling me, stoned in the euphoria of hunger, haunted the halls and their paintings of rocks and trees.

After a one-night stand that spread into a second, I stumbled out onto Central Park West from the apartment of some man, or boy, in a band. I can't remember his name but am struck by the fact that he lived in such gentility. I skulked through the museum's bright rooms with their sacred hush and stood in my black dress before *Trees by the Brookside*; *Group of Trees*; *Sunday Morning* (more trees); *Sunset*; *Landscape, Sunset*; *Study from Nature: Rocks and Trees in the Catskills*; *Study From Nature: Rocks and Trees*; *Autumn Woods*; *Haying at the Edge of the Woods*; *Catskill Study*; *Black Birches, Catskill Mountains*; *Trees in the Catskills* . . . So many trees, rocks, woods, and sunsets. There were places too, Shokan and Shandaken, whose names were yet a mystery, plus moss and rocks and peeling paper birch with threads of golden light gleaming through the picture plane. It was painting like Ruskin advised: truth in nature. They all provided a balm, though I was unsure then what they were curing or soothing.

I was also then still a lonely suburban goth teen dropped into the city, my sensibility trained on the past.

I wore Victorian mourning capes and Edwardian walking suits, LARPing before LARP.

———

I now inhabit those early Victorian paintings I studied in college. One rainy day in New York City after we move, I go to the Met to see them. It is a soggy Thursday in September. Whipped by wind and rain, I clamber up the grand granite staircase. It has the look of an ancient temple. Under the pillars and portico, people force their umbrellas shut. Water runs in rivulets off of us, and we line up before guards at folding tables, presenting our bags like so many offerings. Inside the Great Hall, our voices rise against the marble in a chorus.

I rush past rooms of medieval armor and a courtyard with Tiffany windows, to galleries filled with paintings of here. Of home, of where I live. I stand before a mountain David and I have climbed. Five little cows and a tiny couple fishing are arrayed in the corner of the composition. Around me the room echoes with people. The couple is so small, they're barely a smudge. A woman in a red suit studies the didactic text on the wall. A guard stands in the corner. An older couple, an actual couple, say: "Where is Olive?" "No idea," the man answers. He is in tan. Olive is a name on the wall. It is where the mountain is. It is a township near mine. The woman's hair crests in gray immoveable waves.

Something strange happens in the hum of these voices—the voices behind me and the couple in the painting and the older couple. Soon all the people in all the paintings are talking to me.

The figures are a blur and the voices blend. One woman, an actual flesh-and-blood IRL woman, demands: "Shokan, Ashokan. Where's that? Shandaken?"

Ashokan is the name of the mountain and of the New York City reservoir that sits at its base. Sun glistens on the stream in the canvas. Driving past, I'll catch glimpses of silvered water in the light. At the top blueberries flourish in August. They taste of synesthesia as the gallery goes bitter and sweet.

The gray-cresting-hair woman asks again about Olive. The woman in red says, "I'm going upstate for the weekend. How do I get there?" She gestures at the painting. An enormous gold frame surrounds it. Spotlights glare. Gilt scrolls and scallops encroach on the corners of the canvas. "I am in New York for business and I'm taking my daughter. Where is this? I am from Alabama, and I came to the Met to see these places."

They have all come to the museum to see where I live. This place is freighted with a grand vision of our country. The paintings set the scene for some national sense of identity and Manifest Destiny. I think of a car ad I found a few years ago in the *New Yorker*. "Buick Summer Sell-Down," trumpeted in big, drop-shadow letters. I tore the page from the magazine. The five vehicles—SUVs and sedans—are arrayed before a range of mountains. The light is dramatic, the message: these cars deliver you to a wild and untamed landscape, that dream of America. The past is not done, not over.

The woman in red has a rental car waiting, she says, to all of us in the gallery.

—

Each summer in August the neighboring town of Andes marks the shoot-out in the corral. It doesn't say that's what it's honoring. It's called Community Day and avoids mentioning the murder. Instead the celebration is all flags and marching bands, kids and floats. A tractor dance is set to the *Blue Danube Waltz*. Diggers delicately touch the ground with their buckets as if in a pas de deux. Meanwhile there is modern dance in the park, and some years men parade in calico and paisley dresses and masks. Paintings of masked figurines are stuck in the grass. The parade never really explains the outfits. The men in dresses cavort, circling and spinning as if thrilled to be leering at the crowd. Someone calls them "Calico Indians," and I have no idea what that means.

The years the men cavort, you hear shopkeepers say later that the disguises scare people. This is not the message the businesses want to send. Many years none of the men march at all. The parade marks a rent strike that became a "war." It is called the Anti-Rent War, and there is a long history of strikes like this. This one spreads up and down the Hudson and is the end of a landed aristocracy in America.

The men in dresses are a paisley paramilitary.

———

I look up "rent strike" and find in the *New York Times* in 1932:

REDS BATTLE POLICE IN RENT STRIKE RIOT; 500, Backed by 4,000 Neighbors, Resist Eviction of Seventeen Families in the Bronx. ALL RESERVES CALLED OUT Many Are Pummeled in Melee and Eight Are Arrested, but Court Frees Five. DISPUTE FINALLY SETTLED Trouble Follows Denial of Demand for 15% Reduction -- Cuts of $2 to $4 a Month Are Accepted.

The paper reports on the crowd that shows up, five hundred protesters supported by another four thousand people. They all turn out to protect seventeen families. They are in a section of town the paper calls "the Communist quarter," and I love that there even is a Communist quarter, with a capital C. Studded with the paper's stiff language of "ill-feeling against the police, landlords and city marshals" and "REDS battling," the article is also funny. What amazes me though is how here in the depths of the Depression, the same year my mother's family loses their home in Akron, all these people show up to support their neighbors in the Bronx. They tie their plights together. A month later the paper reports another rent strike with the same demands. Here "at 6 a.m. a man marched up and down the street, blowing a ram's horn, arousing the residents," while others bang on doors, calling, "We need the women to come out and sock the cops." Another woman bites the landlord's chauffeur, and I want to embrace these women with their alliterative *cop-socking*, as well as their civil disobedience, not to mention the man who is out before dawn in late February's damp cold with his ram's horn, which is maybe a shofar? In Biblical times, the instrument was sounded in celebration and to announce the start of a jubilee year when all debts are forgiven.

—

During World War I, women in Glasgow use flour bombs and pull down men's trousers, the bailiffs' trousers, as officials try to deliver eviction notices. The strikes spread across the city. The women also band together and toss the men into the trash at the back of the tenements.

Or, Pauline Newman, sixteen years old, a Lithuanian immigrant. She has fled pogroms and read Marx. She leads a rent strike of 10,000. "Fight the landlord like you fight the czar." That is 1907 on the Lower East Side.

The Highland Land League goes on land raids and battles the police and army. The crofters take on the lairds, the landlords, who over the previous century have burned people out of their homes. Most have fled. Some to the Catskills—why Scottish accents are overheard at the shoot-out. By the 1880s the few left in the Highlands have the smallest and worst bits of land to farm. Crofting was a centuries-old tradition of communal agriculture all under a clan chieftan, until come the 1780s when those chiefs become lords—and landlords—when they realize there's more money in sheep than people, and more prestige in deer parks. The crofters stop paying rent and appropriate land as they see fit. They cull the landlord's deer and sheep. Their slogan: "The people are mightier than a lord."

—

Or here. This war, the Anti-Rent War, is one of the first moments of rural populism in the United States. It begins in 1839 and spreads east to west, eventually throughout the Catskills. Farmers live under patroons, the word a holdover from Dutch colonization. It is the title for the landed aristocracy. The richest, Stephen van Rensselaer's leases are drawn up generations earlier by Alexander Hamilton himself to keep tenants tied to the land. Now Van Rensselaer dies. He is one of the dozen wealthiest Americans of all time according to *New York Times* and *Fortune* and other publications who keep such lists of the rich. He owns all of two counties, Albany and Rensselaer, and part of a third across the Hudson River. The Livingston family owns the rest of that, plus, with the Verplancks, most of the Catskills. The country is gripped by a depression called a "panic," the Panic of 1837, and Stephen Van Rensselaer's sons are desperate to collect rent. He has 100,000 tenants. They do not have the resources to pay. Every year the rent—payable in wheat—goes up, and the soil gets poorer because of over-farming, so the tenants do not have enough for their own subsistence.

The uprising begins as a country doctor named Smith Boughton, who fought in Canada's Patriots' War, delivers petitions to the state assembly. Thousands have signed. They want legislators to outlaw landlords' tenures but fail to get the law changed. Farmers go on rent strike. They vow to strike for a decade if that's what it takes, and across more than a half dozen counties, the protest spreads and becomes the Anti-Rent War. James Fennimore Cooper takes the landowners' side and writes pro-rent treatises. Smith Boughton leads this militia with their lurid masks: hawk-nosed, cockeyed, mouths as gashes of red cloth. He becomes "Big Thunder." That's his fighting name. His first rally ends with a song about tarring and feathering landlords and sheriffs. The Anti-Renters proclaim: "The land is free saith the Lord."

———

On the streets in Andes sometimes the men dance and sometimes the business owners forbid it. Each year, however, the county sheriff puts out a press release marking the line-of-duty death of Osman Steele, undersheriff in 1845.

Chapter 5

AT FIRST RECOVERING "MY HEALTH" comes in walking, and I traipse out of the village and up Pakatakan. In the snow it's like sliding through feathers. Other routes take me along the river and up hills. On one such journey I meet Steve Miller. He's standing by the road clad in red flannel and leaning at an odd angle into a tree. It is early March—the first year in the queenly home. The roadsides are clotted with old gritted snow. I've wandered past the cemetery, a place I like. I can be with the dead and stare at names in rock: Vermilya, Delameter, Gavette, Hendricks; people who as yet mean nothing to me.

I realize this man is reaching for a pail, and dozens of them hang on trees, for sap, maybe. Behind him a white house sits proudly on the brow of a hill. Invoking my dad's ease in speaking to strangers, I call up to him and ask if he's making maple syrup. He stands on the rise, and I am too far away to make out much more than his glasses and the flash of a grin as he raises the bucket. He calls out that he's collecting for a neighbor in the village who still does it the old way. But, he waves at trunks behind him strung with plastic IV tubes, a hospital of trees. That's his sugar bush. Come over, he says. Anytime there's smoke, we're boiling.

———

I also keep heading up Bull Run, to the clearing with its SURGE MILKER and its waterfall. Reaching the high meadow, there is always that shining sensation I had that first day seeing across the land, a fleeting feeling of joy and place. Maybe it's the exertion and being out of breath, some kind of athletic high. The view stuns me. It cuts clear across to the top of Pakatakan, and for a moment I can pretend this is some soaring valley in the Alps. One time a couple is on the porch of the tiny farmhouse there. They are Hank and Muriel. He has a round face and a fondness for cigars, she bobbed hair like my mom. The farm is called the Scott Farm. She is a Scott, or was one, but is now a Robinson.

People here can count in two times; we live in the Bloodgood House, for the owners before the owners who sold to us. Time here is tied to capitalism, to property ownership.

Muriel grew up on the farm. She went to the central school with Steve Miller and his wife Jane. The lines of her life are familiar, though: DC suburbs, government jobs, involvement in nonprofits, kids my age. Hank worked for NOAA as a meteorologist, and she was a bookkeeper for the Audubon Society. My mother was a bookkeeper too, and like her, Muriel talks about birds and wild berries. She gives us permission to pick blackberries on her land in a special spot she has up the road, on a tiny track, an abandoned lane. This is where the best ones are found, she promises. This is where she picked them as a child.

A few months later, Muriel emails that, with all my walking, David and I should use the farm paths and logging roads, woods, and meadows. Just off an old track in a grove of apple trees we find some stone foundations. One is twice my height: a single retaining wall puzzled together from monumental rocks and boulders. It looks like it was once the side of a banked barn. The other is a shed. Its walls are collapsing in on themselves, and it is filled with rusted barrel hoops, old milk cans, and galvanized steel buckets with brown rot where the center has fallen away. It is the sort of trash that would thrill me as a child when I played "Old-Fashioned Days" with my best friend and already dreamt of living in the past and wanted to be Amish when I grew up.

———

This rambling is transcendent and transporting, like Thoreau writes about with his *sans terres* in the essay "Walking." In it he lays out his etymology of "saunter," possibly from *Sainte Terre*—the saints of the land who were walking to the holy land, or else these sans terres, without land. Which make them saints to him, those at home anywhere. He does not believe they were indigent or begging. He dismisses the idea that it had anything to do with poverty. I think too of Harriet Martineau, another Victorian writer and walker. She is a protofeminist and atheist and sociologist, the sorts of *ists* women are not allowed back in the 1830s and 40s. She has walked five hundred miles across Scotland, has been vigorous and engaged and then falls ill, with a mystery sickness that sounds familiar, like a cloud hanging over her; impossible, global, environmental— everything. She tries mesmerism to cure it, and walking, she slowly begins to get her health back as a way of returning to her life, to life.

—

I will walk from Muriel's land to New York City land, some 500 acres the city owns, just past her property line. The parcel is ostensibly to protect the watershed, but no streams run through it, no water, no wetlands, no ponds, rivers, or lakes, just forest. In the winter David I climb up an old lane to a ridge. The ridge is named Kettle Hill. I struggle uphill in my snowshoes, sinking into the deep drifts. It's five degrees but I'm sweating with exertion. The snow squeaks underfoot, like Styrofoam being crushed. The wind bites my cheeks, and as I get closer and closer to this mythic New York, there is not a sound—no cars, traffic, trains or taxis, no planes or horns—just one lone woodpecker, echoing against a tree. The hemlocks' boughs are laced with snow, and I feel as if I'm passing through some magical kingdom. In a sense I am, one where you can seemingly bend the laws governing space and time and find New York City 150 miles from Times Square.

Up here is nothing, or what might be called nothing—just a posted sign and a slender line of old barbed wire growing into the bark of a tree. Neither of us asks if we'll cross it. A feeling rises in my chest and throat—tightness, fear, elation. We step over the metal, clumsy in our snowshoes. Hemlocks tower above, as if a different dream of Manhattan.

—

John Burroughs, a nature writer from the Catskills, talks of walking in his 1875 essay "The Exhilarations of the Road." He has this idea of ambling as freedom, maybe something to counter capitalism or shake off money and some need for clear rewards, for attaining obvious means and ends. He says that walking isn't native to us Americans. "We expect rapid and extraordinary returns. We would make the very elemental laws pay usury." Hence, for most walking is too slow.

Burroughs grows up in Roxbury, just a few miles north of me, and is friends when he's young with Jay Gould, also from Roxbury, who will go on to become a robber baron and railway magnate. Burroughs becomes close to Henry Ford and Thomas Edison, so clearly there are some ends

and means here in his worldview. He becomes more cele-
brated than the president, even. On a whistle-stop tour
with Teddy Roosevelt, everyone turns out for Burroughs,
who is now virtually unknown. He's kind of an awful
writer too. That piece on walking begins with an ode to
the bare foot that is strange and sensual. He "brags lustily,"
he says, about this unshod foot:

> I catch a glimpse of the naked human foot.
> Nimbly it scuffs along, the toes spread, the sides
> flatten, the heel protrudes; it grasps the curbing,
> or bends to the form of the uneven surfaces—a
> thing sensuous and alive, that seems to take
> cognizance of whatever it touches or passes. [. . .]
> It looks a little repulsive; but it is beautiful for all
> that. Though it be a black foot and an unwashed
> foot, it shall be exalted.

But, he opens the essay with a quote from Walt Whitman.
When everyone hates Whitman—too queer and idiosyn-
cratic, un-Victorian and immodest, too much sex and lust
and love for others—Burroughs champions him. And,
Burroughs calls walking "a more vital co-partnership."

—

Now here I am standing with David in spring in NYC, on
a hill, a ridge, as if we have stepped over a boundary into
the unknown: evergreens, moss, and ferns.

—

David is nervous to go to Steve Miller's, nervous to impose.
Shy and British, the kind of British raised working class

and told to keep his place, he worries about whether we were really invited.

In the sap house, steam fogs our glasses. It smells of burning sugar and wood. Steve's wife Jane and her sister and brother-in-law stand around a fire so hot we stack coats and hats, mittens and gloves by the door. Steve is wearing the same flannel shirt as before, and his square glasses make his face, soft, softer. His hair has gone bald with wisps of gray like down. Jane has chestnut hair cut close, and even though she barely knows us, her voice encircles us in its warmth.

The sap boils down, and, anxious, I talk too much. David grows quieter. I talk more. There is a mention of politics. Jane says something of the forever wars or midterm elections or health insurance and how lucky we are to have the NHS in London. A fizzy feeling rises. It is partly the heat, but also I assumed everyone from here, who stayed here, has to be a Republican. Despite the stories my dad has told, the news has a narrative of rural and Republican being coequal, and I have believed this narrative.

In writing you're told to have round characters, people who defy expectations. The idea being that you, the reader, get to know someone, and everyone has contradictions that make them seem more real. Here are the people who become real to me.

David loads wood into the stove. The task keeps him from having to speak much. He ventures a question about Steve's woodlot, and then his log splitter and his trees. Foam bubbles in the syrup. Jane drops in a dab of butter and explains it dispels the froth. In writing, the round character often displaces their feelings onto objects that give us insights into their emotions and motivations.

—

As we walk home from Steve and Jane's that day in the sap house, I bob ahead and back. My footsteps echo on the frozen road. Do you like them? I like them. I repeat the question insistently because I need David to affirm their connection to us, because I have talked too much and he has been so quiet and I want him to forgive me.

Yes, he says in his laconic voice, with his soft accent. I do. Like parents, he says. Or the parents we'd have if we were from here.

—

Writers use displacement to show a character's feelings— those that might even be unknown to the character themselves. Instead the emotions are placed onto an object—a pigeon, say, or a rock—making it clear how a character feels without an author's telling us directly.

Another writer would describe David at Steve and Jane's woodstove. David would in this account study the scabbed gray bark of the cherry log and touch its red-orange heartwood. These would hold his nervousness. The log's rings would grow tighter and tighter, his heart loosening with his focus. There would be the stiff leather work gloves he dons to load the firebox. The heat at his face as he opens the stove. It reflects orange, licking flames on his skin and glasses. The glove's seams would be rough. He'll concentrate on them. I want to slow down on those details because of how much I love him. To linger on them is to linger on his touch.

—

Muriel has been selling some of the farm's acreage. She has a deal set but pulls out at the last minute. The buyer wants covenants in the deed forbidding people from walking their dogs on the land. I don't know the full story, but it's something that strikes her as ridiculous, this idea that you can't cross the land or walk on the paths or that dogs can't run free in the country. It sounds like what my mother would say.

Reader, we buy the land, the one with the foundations, the side of the barn, and the tumble-down remains of a shed. It is early 2008. We don't have the money to purchase it, and it takes us more than a year even to make an offer. I am too embarrassed, I tell Hank and Muriel, to try. What we can pay is pitiful and would shame us all, I say as we sit in her kitchen eating pie. Instead, Muriel lowers the price and holds the note. That also feels significant. It is a private sale because no bank will finance vacant land, not even early in 2008 when banks seem to finance anything. In this, she and Hank come to feel like parents, like my parents, a tribute to how much we want to fit, to how much longing our belonging hides.

———

Now stand with me on a rutted lane that runs up nearly to the ridgeline and peters out. There is a new beaver pond and an old hayfield rising against the trees. They hide meadows where cows once roamed. Maple, birch, and aspen encroach, and in the woods we find tiny saffron salamanders, some as small as my thumbnail. The land is encircled by abandoned dairy farms. On the other side are those 500 acres cleaved from two farms now part of New York City.

I start to write for the local paper, and I often hear talk about the city. One neighbor up the road says she'd never have sold to us, would never break up land like that, not to the city, not to anyone. She is fierce in this and has no doubt that Muriel's father would have been as well. People talk about feudal powers, how the city can buy land, any land, to protect its water. *They don't want us here. The city just wants to regulate us out of existence. They're waiting for the day to get us all off—for a flood big enough to get rid of the town entirely.* There is talk too of tyranny and absentee landlords and the city as a land baron. Someone says something about a war, a rent war, and that year two people, two senators, a Black man and a white woman, both of whom would be firsts if they win, run for president. On the news: so many pictures of suburbs and new homes all shades of perfect cream. They materialize against deserts and dirt lots or lawns verdant with newly-rolled sod. Later the grass browns because there is no one to water, because the homes have been foreclosed upon.

—

And, the land here looks like a dream, like those nineteenth-century paintings with their stirring landscapes of solitary mountains, or mountain streams and their waterfalls, or boulders graced by golden light piercing through birch boughs—all because of the city and its vast empty parcels of fields and forest. Everywhere the soil is so poor, studded with so much stone, there's a saying for it: "Two rocks for every dirt." The dirt feels like destiny as the trees grow into the fields and stone walls snake up old lanes to nowhere. What else were people supposed to have done with all that stone but build walls?

—

That summer my parents' financial planner phones and offers us something called a HELOC to build on the land. I hear the word first as heal-lock, an acronym of healing and locking. I have no idea it's a credit line against the house with a turret named for two queens. He explains it's possible to borrow money, interest only, he stresses, because the house's value has, he says, obviously gone up. If we want to build on the land, we can use that capital from our home. It's no risk, he assures us. We won't owe any interest unless we use this healing and locking money. We have, though, Muriel's loan on the land and a note on our house, so more credit, more money even in interest payments alone, seems impossible. So too is getting this call and all the privilege that implies. Because of my parents we are being offered this money.

Still, we accept the Healing and Locking. We leave the money untouched, too nervous to try and pay more down on more debts each month. Instead, on the land we put up the canvas tent. It's a wall tent like soldiers used in the Civil War. It has a pitched roof, suggesting the platonic ideal of a home, and inside is a bed, woodstove, and a desk.

—

Now picture the scene. On the land it is dusk, summer. The tent is high on the hill and we—you, David, and I, walk down through the field. It is late July. The meadow is dotted with milkweed in bloom. Monarchs flit past. We sit on the bank by the beaver pond and search for any sign of the animals, sure a ripple in the water must be one, maybe a baby. Only it is nothing, then something, a brownbody-brownwaterbrownglide. It gets closer and closer. David films it on his camera—cell phones have yet to film video and even if they did, there is no cell coverage here. A head pops up to watch us from the water. Seconds, a minute, pass; the air is still. Cirrus clouds shimmer with the last of the light. David's camera makes a dink as he stops recording. The beaver claps its tail and disappears, and we're happy to have it even acknowledge our presence.

———

Over time, along the banks the water gets higher and higher, the ground soggier and soggier. A tree disappears. The chiseled stump is all that remains, and that too is swallowed by water. Each time we come there are more twigs, more mud, the dam rising. It takes months to realize the beavers are building a terraced chain of ponds to increase their terrain. I become obsessed with them.

They are the rodent socialists of the animal world, allowing mice and muskrats and frogs to share their home, even the food. The system, I think, is collective, cooperative, utopian . . . Beavers transform a landscape more than any other creature except humans. Here, along this stream they've made a long, flat plane. They have come and gone from this spot probably for centuries. They will move on again after eating the willow saplings. The pond will drain and disappear, leaving more grass to wave in the wind.

———

One trip back to see my parents—my dad has just been discharged from the hospital—they tell David and me the story of moving to DC. The tale is familiar in its outlines if not the details. It sounds random and impossible, but apocryphal and leading to the future, one that gives birth to all that we have and I am in their lives.

My dad in this telling is in a bar in Oneonta in 1953. Oneonta is the town where I go to the doctor's in a ghost mall turned medical complex. My father is out with the manager of another co-op, this one based in in my county.

Sitting in the dining room, I listen to my mom and watch my father. He nurses a cup of tea gone cold. A sweater drifts around his shoulders, and I worry he is exhausted. We each occupy our places at the table, where we've sat for decades. It has witnessed my teenaged fights, first steps, and first solid food. David is in the guest spot, usually stacked with unread copies of the *New York Times*. My dad is taciturn and quiet, like David. They say you marry your parents.

My mom recounts the events, my father in this bar. She leaves a pause for laughter because he will become someone who even now just out of the hospital never skips his evening drink. His juice and vodka, though, is barely sipped, the ice cubes long melted. The glass sits perspiring next to his tea.

In the story my parents get a call from the person soon to become my father's employer. Only they don't really get the call. They don't have a phone. They can't afford a phone. This soon-to-be employer who leads a national group of co-operatives manages to get hold of a neighbor.

This soon-to-be employer is also a former congressman. My parents' neighbor finds my mom. My mom relays the name of the bar; former congressman calls the bar, and now at the table I feel like I can touch my parents' lives. I picture the rust belt town and its depleted Main Street, and see one place there, the Red Jug, derelict and sad. In the bar, I hear noise and men and darkness. On the phone the former congressman offers my dad a job. He says no, he'll have to come down to interview and meet them in person. This former congressman holds his hand over the receiver and asks whoever is nearby, This guy Kabat wants to come down and meet. Should I bring him in?

They do.

At this point in the story, at the table, my dad beams. He was good at negotiation but so poor he has no suitcase. He carries his things in a box. They put him up at a fancy hotel a few blocks from the White House, and after the interview the two men stand near Dupont Circle. The former representative says, So, you'll take the job right? My father says he'll have to discuss it with his wife. Of course, the assumptions are that husbands' careers will trump everything.

Now in the retelling my dad takes over the story. Each week, he says animatedly, every few days, the former congressman calls, offering more money, more benefits. Finally my father agrees, which is how I come to be a child more than a quarter century later, born into the suburbs of Washington, DC, with roots that hail back to the foothills of the mountains where I live now. He devotes his life to co-ops, and my mom is soon cast into a life simply as "the wife."

Chapter 6

RECENTLY A GRAD STUDENT OF mine, a painter who is more a friend than student at this point, sends around a Walt Whitman poem "To a Stranger" for us to discuss in class. I'm teaching a class on place, and her response is this: that place is this moment between people, between strangers, an ever-shifting chance of possibility and connection. Kinship. The ship, that bridge, to the stranger.

> Passing stranger! you do not know how longingly I look
>   upon you,
> You must be he I was seeking, or she I was seeking, (it
>   comes to me as of a dream,)

She also sends a Carter Family song that goes, "Hello, stranger, put your loving hand in mine." The line repeats, and this love is the thing in the hand, in the trust. "You are a stranger and you're a pal of mine."

The next line has the singer picking up a drunkard to care for them.

And Whitman: "I am to see to it that I do not lose you."

His next poem begins: "This moment yearning and thoughtful sitting alone . . ."

And, I stare out the sunroom window. The village mayor walks her dog. Hello, stranger.

—

In the house with a turret, winters come and go. I am now so far from the London doctor, from the drab, from the oatmeal, from the allergies, from my "health," that I am outside on a mountaintop when it is two degrees. The cold air stings my lungs. Snow crystals twinkle, casting prisms of light. I am skiing. I have become someone who can speed down steep slopes at velocity, and I become friends with Rudd. We meet on a chairlift.

Here are the strangers adopting each other, later toasted over beers in the lodge. People will press close to our bar stools. A band plays old-time country music. Someone says, "Rudd, Rudd-this, Rudd-that." Another: "Rudd I've not seen you in—" "Rudd how's the—" "Rudd, we should . . ." Rudd, his name electric in their mouths. I don't know these people. He introduces me. A halo of attention shifts to my shoulders. I have on an orange knit hat to hide my tangled hair.

He and his brothers run a construction company from their family farm. They build roads and culverts and raise highland cattle. He also restores creeks and streams. The brothers sell cuts of beef and pork and eggs by the dozen in the same store where they sell Husqvarna chain saws, chaps, and gloves, where David will come to buy a chain saw. The place smells of sawdust and motor oil.

On the chairlift I tell him that I've heard his name "Rudd Hubbell" spoken by so many with such reverence— the syllables slung low and long together—that he sounds hallowed. He speaks with his words chewed down to nubs. I tell him the way people mention him, I assumed he was old.

Well, I am, he says, a good-old boy.

But he is not old. He is about my age, and one of the first friends my age here. He is as slight and small as David and has bright gray-green eyes, a sparkle of trouble. Sometimes he wears a beard, sometimes not. He does however always wear the same pair of worn brown Carhartts and gray wool cap and rubber L.L.Bean boots no matter the season.

———

Now below us on the slope, someone yips, calling out in glee. Rudd asks why I moved here, and I don't even mention being sick.

Rime flocks the tips of trees. Whites and grays rise against each other from ground to sky. On the chairlift I point out a vireo nest dangling from a branch.

On the next chairlift ride, he asks my take on the town and its issues. The question takes me aback. I've seen the "Save the Locals" stickers and absorbed the dictum of how you might live here your whole life and never fit. There is the us and them, city people, flatlanders, and all the things said about those not from here, how they come with ideas to change things.

I answer earnestly, I remember that, but not what I say, only that I'm surprised he's asking. He says, being new, you'll have a new perspective. What strikes me now is that he's interested at all.

———

Other people become kin—Steve and Jane, Muriel and the godfathers. In the word "kinship," the ship is a bridge between kin and something like kin. The ship is my hope for connections—like with parataxis how I see all as connected.

Or, I want it to be. The thing about kinship is that it says you're not related but trying to be. You are like family but not actually family at all. It's that thing of the "like," or likening, of similes. Sometimes they are more powerful because they are trying to leap over differences to build bonds.

———

The trips down to my parents' become more urgent. They happen in the middle of the night or the afternoon or the break of day. The time of emergencies is never set to a clock or calendar or convenience. Things are thrown into a bag, the bag thrown into the car. I try to drive eighty-five miles per hour straight through the entire state of Pennsylvania. There are falls and emergency rooms, ambulances, 911 calls to firemen who offer lifting assistance when my mom can't get my father up. Once he trips over a houseplant, a prickly cactus called a crown of thorns, and nearly falls through the plate glass windows across the front of the house. He is airlifted to a shock-trauma unit.

I sit by bedsides, freeze meals, and whatever I do pales to my sisters' efforts. They live nearby and will rush to wait with my mom at the hospital. The next day when I arrive, I'll drive her there, talk to doctors, take notes— and I don't realize my father is dying. Or, I don't let myself. No doctor ever says that this is it, this is what death looks like: these trips, these falls, the hospital stays and rehab, the transfusions, the scans, the emergency room where my mom is there until 4 a.m. before my father will be admitted. Instead I search for others as substitute parents, the godfathers, Steve and Jane, Hank and Muriel, but I don't see what I am losing in my own family, not yet. Or, that the yet is now.

———

That visit to my parents' when my mom tells us the story of moving to Washington, she gives me a plant, a wax plant, with glossy dark-green leaves on long tendrils. A dairy farmer's wife, the board secretary, gave it to my parents as a leaving present to take to their new life as they left the co-op. Their car was packed with houseplants. My parents left in a blizzard, ran off the road into a snowbank and abandoned the car. They took Squeaky the cat and stayed in a motel. All the other plants died. The wax plant was the only one that survived the move.

I wish I could say the way she gifts it to me is special or endowed with meaning because I now live nearby. Instead she is frustrated and angry: You take these plants or I'm throwing them away. I don't have the energy anymore.

———

She knows what this one symbolizes. Only a sprig survived, and she coaxed it back to life. When it blooms in summer, she'd point to its exquisite flowers like carved wax and tell the story of its perseverance. Now it sits in the sunroom with me, where I write, so too the crown of thorns that nearly killed my father.

———

Steve and Jane's house, I learn, is a recreation of his parents' place. It was flooded out by the reservoir for New York City's water in the early 1950s. His parents built this one after being forced to move. A sign, UNION GROVE POST OFFICE, hangs on the porch. His mom had been the postmaster. Steve and Jane live in the outlines of his parents' lives, collecting sap, making syrup, cutting wood.

Steve's first home in Union Grove is now under water. Watching the engineers build the reservoir, he decides he wants to be an engineer himself. He works on New York's last interstate that runs from Albany to the Pennsylvania border. Now he is retired. His daughter is a hydrologist. There is something still for me to learn about recreations, outlines and the patterns of lives. I study an image of him and his mother, Agnes, outside the original house—before the flood, before the loss, before the move.

Before we buy the land, Steve and Jane come look at it with us. He mows a suitable site for building. They also have the same plant, a wax plant, from his parents' original home. It hangs in their living room and has grown into the woodwork and curtain rail and can never be moved. It is bound into the house.

Chapter 7

THERE ARE HAZY PICTURES OF my parents kissing, she with Veronica Lake hair flipped from her face. But hers is brown, not bottle blonde. In another, the two of them lie in the grass holding hands. He grins. She laughs.

As she kisses him, she cranes her neck. He looks down, abashed, and smiles. In the background you can just make out a blur of a woman. She swirls away in a dress, a spectral vision caught on film. My mom is not in a dress or heels. She is barefoot. The kissing is at Oberlin, the grass-lying in Upstate New York. My parents are both impossibly young.

She was born Lois. The name is devout, pious, and comes into English with the Reformation, those wanting direct covenants with God, though her parents never go to church. At Oberlin she becomes Sandy. It is a portmanteau of her first and second names, Lois Ann, said together—the S and Ann slurred into one, "Sann." She is a self-creation, a new person who leaves behind family, the factories, dirt farms, and eating weeds in the Depression because the family is so poor; most of all she leaves her mother, who criticizes everything she does. Instead Sandy sounds masculine and new. It is independent, and she is too.

——

She's the one who teaches me the names of plants and wildflowers when I am little. Butter and eggs, a miraculously miniature yellow snapdragon in fields, and bladder campions with white bonnets; pearly everlastings that dried look exactly the same as alive. And, boneset. I'm seven, maybe eight, when she shows it to me. My canvas sneakers have grown wet in a marshy meadow. The plant rises past my hips to my chest, and the name is alive as a secret. I ask if it fixes bones, and she says people probably once believed that. Now I know it is to cure breakbone fever, agues, and viruses.

Its fuzzy, frilled flowers lift in clusters to the sun. Each year growing up, I scrawled a list of the blooms I find and note the dates, always the dates. They are important, my mom tells me. The words, the names, though, contain worlds. Out on the land now I see the same flowers, and I look up her name Lois: a warrior. It also means *more desirable*.

In Margaretville spring arrives. Behind the tent we hear something like a low motor or a basketball being dribbled close to the ground. We are sure it's a vibration in the tent fly. Maybe the wind. What else could it be? There is nothing nearby, a rock wall, young forest . . . We mention it to Rudd, and he laughs and tells us we have a lust-crazed grouse, drumming. The bird picks a mossy log and sits upon it, beating his wings to attract a mate. There are also peepers, tiny tree frogs the size of my thumbnail, their chirps like birdsong or crickets, and the birds too are singing in the fields and trees, everyone crying, pounding for sex sex sex.

For a while I attend the Methodist church around the corner from our house. An expat Korean man officiates. In halting English his sermons stake out historical context where Jesus is a radical reformer, a socialist, and not even the first proclaimed a messiah. He's just the one we hear about. The pastor talks too of the Biblical history of Jubilee years, and of how we should forgive all debts, not just as some emotional forgiveness but financial too.

I go to church looking to fit in and find some succor in these sermons, and from being in a room with loggers and laborers, nurses and insurance brokers, all of whose supplications seem more substantial than mine. We sing hymns that promise: "I'll fly away oh glory I'll fly away in the morning."

My parents are confused about this churchgoing. My mother jokes that one daughter's a Buddhist, the other a Methodist? At least one of you, she says of my middle sister who works doing budgets at the Department of Energy, follows the faith of spreadsheets and a government job.

It is a Sunday morning in the church basement with its old linoleum and folding tables and smells of soap and coffee. Over cake and cookies after services and after these promises to fly away, I ask the sole dairy producer left in town about his farm. He talks to me about the price of milk. It is always falling for the farmer but rising in the stores. He looks at the ground and at his Styrofoam cup. He says, I don't know, and that it is hard. He pauses, We are mortgaged to the hilt. A corner is torn from the cups edge where he has been worrying at it.

—

David learns to log our land. He follows HELPP, an acronym for safely felling trees. It stands for plans for hinges and lean and escaping should the tree fall the wrong way, your way, if the tree comes for your life. The acronym also suggests care, and he learns to bring a tree down carefully, exactly. For a man who is a graphic designer and lines everything up on a grid, whose office is far away and whose clients are slowly disappearing in the economic crisis, it is satisfying.

—

In the roads, grit lingers into May. The salt limns the cracks and frost heaves like veins, and in summer cars kick up the dust. On walks I can taste the salt in my throat. That August the Korean pastor marries the godfathers' oldest friends, who moved to Margaretville a few years after them. It is not an actual marriage but a blessing, held outside the church because the church will not recognize gay marriage.

———

All of Margaretville, all of my town and county, and several other counties are part of something called the Hardenbergh Patent. My own county, Delaware County, is the size of a state: Delaware by some estimates, or Rhode Island by others, and all of these acres—thousands and thousands—were part of a land grant. It hearkens back to an era when the United States was not united, not states, but ruled by a queen and then a king. It's a land deal signed twice, in 1706 and then again in 1708 with two different signatures, neither of which belongs to Johannes Hardenbergh. He was a Dutch merchant and county sheriff as well as an officer in the local militia, and he serves as the front man for seven other investors with conflicts of interest that break the law.

The Hardenbergh group includes the attorney general who draws up the documents, making it unseemly if not illegal for him to have a share in the scheme. There's also the surveyor general who's forbidden from benefitting from land deals, and no one knows exactly how much land this patent contained. Maybe two million acres? Maybe one and a half . . . It stretches from the Hudson to the western Catskills and beyond. The Livingstons get in on it in the 1750s with the Verplancks, buying out most of the original investors for pennies on the dollar. The story has one Robert Livingston (a younger son, a second son, the one who won't inherit his family's vast estates) looking across the Hudson and spying mountains for the taking. Everyone believes riches, ore, minerals, and tenants await, none of which has materialized, not yet. Then as white people migrate west, they push out the Munsee Lenape and Oneida and Mohawks, and the settlers come to be tenants.

All around me everyone pays rent. Fifteen thousand of the 20,000 acres in the Lewis Tract that makes up my town are rented out. It is named for Morgan Lewis. He fights in the Revolution and becomes governor of New York State and marries a Livingston. Their daughter is Margaret, the Margaret of Margaretville. He also co-founds NYU where I will soon teach. He is a tenant landlord with holdings on both sides of the Hudson. George Washington meanwhile nearly wins thousands of acres in the Catskills from another Livingston family member in a lottery, a sporting game of chance that the rich fancy back then.

In the Catskills, landlords believe their tenants need to pay rent, that they are too lazy without it, and will only produce enough to get by. I keep thinking about this "laziness." The word comes bound with all the justifications of capitalism: a moral obligation to work harder and earn more. These accusations of laziness appear over and over through the decades to blame the poor and make them culpable in their poverty. I wonder too what is wrong with getting by?

———

When we move to the queenly house with its turret, Lewis and Livingston descendants still own a massive estate straddling two neighboring towns.

———

It is summer. Vacant storefronts loom behind dark glass in the village. FOR RENT signs hang on the doors. People say they'll never get filled, that this is the end of us. A wood turtle walks up Bull Run when the water is low, following a lumbering path. The animal can cover 350 feet a day, which apparently is far for a turtle. We find another crossing the two-lane highway and carry it to the other side. It rushes away, legs scrambling. Their curved, carved shells do look like wood, as the name suggests. In the ice age the turtles moved their territory south, and as the glaciers retreated, came north again in their paths of three-hundred-and-some-feet a day.

On the news that fall, men empty their offices. They wear rumpled shirts and stunned expressions. They clutch boxes with binders and photos and look like they have never picked up anything in their lives. Steve Miller says the crisis will not be here, not like that; our region is too poor for the kind of property speculation we see on TV.

The house with a turret and two names is valued at less than we paid for it, but is still worth more than we owe. We hear words too on the news, "underwater," as if a flood. We cross the border to Pennsylvania to campaign for a person promising Hope. We go door-to-door in a town built on coal mining, and David asks, What will people think? He is not a US citizen, not yet, and has a British accent. He has never canvassed in his life, never knocked on a stranger's door to plead a candidate's case. That is not how campaigns happened in the UK. Average people do not do this. In my family we always do, and this year we talk about how heartbreaking it is that my Black uncle died the year before and does not get to vote for the historic candidate and for Hope.

In the coal town, foreclosure notices are wheat-pasted

and taped to windows and doors, sometimes stapled to plywood affixed over windows and doors. The signs announce: BY ORDER OF or SPECIAL PROCEEDINGS and NOTICE OF FORECLOSURE SALE. For those, NOTICE is in all caps, framed on both sides by images of a sheriff's badge. *Help!!* someone spray-painted across their siding. At some houses it feels as if they've been abandoned in a hurry. They are empty but for a stray shoe or a kid's toy. One has a pink quilt hanging from a broken window. We leave our bag of election literature on the door handle.

Sheriff's Department

NOTICE TO VACATE

Case Number: _____

Judgment debtor, member's of the judgment debtor's household, and any occupants residing with the judgment debtor

By virtue of a Writ of Possession of Real Property, a copy of which is attached

YOU ARE ORDERED TO VACATE THE PREMISES DESCRIBED IN THE WRIT NO LATER THAN:

_____20_____

Rudd says that most of the mortgages here are from local banks, which won't bundle and sell on their loans. On Main Street more windows go empty. Some have FOR RENT signs and others no signs. That November after the first snow falls and melts away, the grit glitters in the streets. People talk about how the city is relieved; it can't wait for us to disappear. And yet, in my town and village and county, Hope wins.

———

The 1837 recession, this capital-P "Panic," is caused by a real estate boom and bust, loose lending then banks tightening credit. A property bubble bursts, fueled by foreign speculation. There's been a tech boom, only this technology is factories, faster production, lower wages, cheaper goods. As things cost less, less money is earned.

Banks call in loans to cover their depleted reserves and raise interest rates. The media drums up fear—this media is newspapers. There are countless of them, penny papers: the *Huge Paw*, *Log Cabin*, *Whig Star*, and *Williamsburg Democrat*. They are cheap and partisan, as common as social media today. There are also no press ethics, no standing on truth or facts or fact-checking.

On TV after the election for Hope, I hear that the candidates from both parties feared everyone would rush to banks and ATMs to take out all of their money, and there would be no money to withdraw, and the banks would fail.

In 1837, banks do fail. Investors lose their nerve. A hundred million is lost in New York alone; businesses go bankrupt. In the United States wheat crops fail too, and hunger spreads.

With the free-trade market economy, the idea is that in raising interest rates, the invisible hand will fix everything. This money will return to where it will make money with the higher rates. Things do not turn out that that way in the 1830s. More banks go under. The collapse spreads. It is one of the first international depressions.

And in the United States, technology does not free the workers. Industrial revolutions haven't brought the revolution people need, just factories, where those forced off the land into the city by the failing wheat harvests seek work. Wages continue to plunge as the recession spreads. Immigrants arrive. They come to escape tyranny, the start of famines across Northern Europe, as well as this Panic that has tracked across Europe. Instead people get race-to-the-bottom employment and anti-immigrant violence.

———

One morning David gets a call from my parents' financial advisor. The advisor doesn't ask for me. He just talks. Things are urgent, he says. We have to act immediately. On the speakerphone I hear him mention the healing and locking. It turns out to be no comfort at all. His institution is closing all outstanding home equity lines, and if we want that money, we better go to our bank branch today.

Cash the checks for the credit line now, this morning, and deposit the money in your accounts.

He says things about negative equity and anxieties higher up. What's clear is that this institution, a national brokerage house, has extended credit lines like ours to countless people, against house values. The bank realizes those values have disappeared and thinks our house value has disappeared. Go this morning, he repeats.

———

In Margaretville people say you can buy drugs at the village bar, called a pub. It's a tiny storefront, the windows covered. The door is graced by a high half-moon of clouded glass impossible to see through. In the paper, the crime blotter reports arrests for heroin and OxyContin. The constable in the next town over, his daughter is arrested. Rudd says, yeah, you can get anything you want there at the pub. Everyone knows.

—

The deer that winter are so ravenous they eat the arborvitae and rhododendron that border the house. Which means the animals stand within breathing distance of us.

—

David is on the phone with his business partner. They talk in low voices. On another call with their accountant, I hear him ask something about their tax liability and can they deduct a client's bad debt? It's noon, and the firehouse alarm sounds, the air raid siren. I have no idea what the bookkeeper says.

Oh yeah, David replies, the world is ending, but this is just the rehearsal. It goes off every day here at lunchtime.

On walks he frets over work. It will take him more than a mile to open up. Climbing the hill past the waterfall and Muriel's, silence wedges between us. He hides his worry, or tries to, but I can feel it vibrate in the air. There is a set to his mouth, a small clench in his check. I study him when I'm sure he won't notice, when I'm sure he is looking down. We'll pass the red barn and a wetland Muriel once said to avoid because of snapping turtles. Slowly he'll start to talk about what's wrong with the business, and his fears, or about his partner and their relationship. Or, about pay. Or, how much equity the partner has taken. Or, the client that has gone under, the one who didn't pay their bills, the printers whose bills are due. Or, how unhappy the partner is that David's far away. We'd thought he could be in two places at once, that what hadn't worked in our six months of courtship might be a long-term plan for his career.

—

I lose work too. The copywriting disappears.

As we walk, I point out the flowers that will dry to defy death and loss. Everlasting, I tell him.

—

Thoreau describes walking as this singular experience of the self in nature where you escape the world's boundaries. That's part of *Walden*, part of "Walking." Of course, this is also the era that lionizes the individual in economics, and he uses the metaphor of property, of surveying—ownership of the land. Thoreau writes about how surveyors bind up the land and tie it to capitalism. These rambles carry him past those lines and fences. He gets this transcendent, open experience.

In walking I find myself also diaphanous, porous. Inside, outside, all my sides are one. David and I trespass; we make it up to New York City, and how to describe this moment? The wind shakes the hemlocks. A hawk cries and circles overhead. Something else vibrates into the moment too, flashing through the boughs like sunlight.

I have called that feeling exercise or endorphins, but it is boundlessness, as if all parts and pores and sex and body are air. I am beginning to cross time. It feels as if the place, this Manhattan on a mountainside, is alive and pulsing, the earth as infinity, the soil, rocks, ground, and mosses reaching through time. Or, maybe it's just the dazzling prisms in the dew this morning.

In his essay Thoreau talks of a miser out with a surveyor, trying to make the land pay, the land as capital. The two search for a landmark—a posthole, he writes, to mark out the property line. In Thoreau's vision, they're "surrounded by devils" and manage to locate the mark, "three little stones where a stake had been driven, and looking nearer, I saw that the Prince of Darkness was his surveyor."

That winter up in New York City on the ridge we find a hunting blind, a platform built from new two-by-fours ten feet up a tree. Nailed to the back are two white plastic Eames chairs. They are pristine, and my heart races. Someone else has intruded on our metropolis. It's no longer our secret. David jokes about a hunter who reads shelter mags while waiting for deer. I think of the Prince of Darkness and violence.

On the side of the platform hangs a shiny steel winch, thick and heavy. My mind flies with the dangers I imagine, what the hook is supposed to hang, to lift. I know it's for gutting deer, but I see something more sinister. We only find the blind once. We look for it over and over, but it's as if it was a chimera, the chairs, the chains, and dangers. In the distance we hear the fire alarm in the village. Coyotes yowl in response. Their calls Doppler off the ridge.

The tree stand inspires the crime novel; so do those rumors of drugs at the bar. The book is not so much that I can write suspense but that I want to write about here, and I find the longer I live here place is a character—or shapes characters. In her writing Hardwick sees place and character as linked, or that maybe place can be the story. Still though, I feel like I need to write to expectations, to an order of plot and chronology, when all I'm really interested in are the land and its revelations.

Chapter 8

IN THE SUNROOM NOW, I study old issues of the local paper: notices about Muriel's father, his barn, a haying bee, her wedding—a double-ring ceremony, a honeymoon in Niagara Falls like her parents had. I read our old emails: she's driving up for the summer; there are plans to come over; she's pleased we're getting the land. When the listing ran out, she says, she didn't think it would sell. She invites us over for wine and canapés to celebrate.

Then, there are plans to take Muriel to the doctors and bring casseroles. I email my mom for recipes. What sort of food is good for chemo? There is chicken soup, and chicken and rice casserole. Next summer, Muriel writes, we'll walk the stream when she is feeling up for it. Her strength is returning. This fall she is feeling good. She has stories about her parents she wants to tell me. She types that she's been tired, but that is temporary she is sure.

It is January. David's company will not survive what is now being called the Great Recession. He has to return to London, and I with him. We'll sleep on the foldout sofa in his office. The morning we are leaving my mother calls at seven. My father fell in the night. I'm still to go, she says. Her voice is frayed with exhaustion. I tell myself David needs me there. From his office in the nook with the sofa, I phone each day and ask if I should return. No one knows; no one's sure. There's pneumonia, maybe some kind of cancer. The words are vague. Everyone says stay, until one day my sister says, "I have no idea. I think you should come home."

My father dies that night. I fly in the morning.

It's February, ten days after my dad's death. I lie in my childhood bedroom. The ancient oak's boughs are silhouetted black overhead. The sky the white of nothing. I try to call Muriel, not for any reason. I just miss her. Hank puts her on. Above me the sky has gone angry and dark. The kids have been. She might make it one more day.

Soon I see ghosts in plants. My mom who is still very much alive abides in the wax plant they were given when they left New York. My dad is in the cactus that he tripped over and then had to be airlifted to the hospital. The wax plant seems to respond to my mother's health, waxing and waning as she declines and recovers.

I sweep the plant leaves up nearly daily in the sunroom looking out over mountain at whose base the Lenape sachem Cacawalemin had lived, had sold the land. The cactus has sharp spikes and poisonous sap. It can burn the skin. The crown of thorns came from Madagascar and was imported into the Middle East before Christ's time. The wax plant is silent. The leaves yellow from too much light.

———

That spring, up picking fiddleheads in New York City, we smell the black stench of rotten meat that crawls into the sinuses. Death. David is sure it's a bird; I think a deer. We track away from the odor and find ourselves nearly on top of a bear spread on its side. Its massive body is soft and splayed out; it looks like it's resting, and near the head is a downed hemlock bough. We're sure the bear was hit by the limb in a windstorm. Two weeks later David returns, and all that is left are its bones. I read that bears' paws can be mistaken for human hands on crime scenes.

A man walks silently with his backpack through the village every day. He never speaks. I wonder where he's going, the hours he wanders, what endurance he's preparing for.

Rudd tells us someone shot the bear; someone several ridges away, seven miles from us, someone who keeps bees for honey. I picture the animal, its height and weight, so big that a bullet doesn't kill it, not at first. The bear picks itself up, lumbering with a wound over that distance, stumbling and dragging itself until finally it collapses and dies alone, here in the green of the hemlocks and ferns.

David and I crash our bikes at a railroad crossing on a highway outside town. David is splayed on the shoulder at an angle that suggests a neck injury. Firefighters descend on the scene. One comes in striped socks, dressed like it's 1900, from a vintage baseball game nearby. My rain+bird is rushed to the hospital, and we are told he'll need to be airlifted out. After scans and X-rays, hours under noisy machines, he is sent home. Outside the turret in an arborvitae, grackles nest. The parents, with their luminous midnight blue heads and white-rimmed eyes, watch me. Their stares are uncanny.

———

Sometime after Muriel dies, I need to know what she was going to tell me. I email Hank. I ask about the rocks and ruins and her parents.

I pester her friends Georgie and Shirley.

Hank emails back:

> I don't know much about the foundations—they were in ruins when I first met Muriel so I don't think anyone lived there in the twentieth century. As a farm, it must have been a leftover from the anti-rent war. It was too small to support much more than a few cows, pigs and those other animals, yet there had to be enough to make the rent for the patroons. Must have been a hard life.

On the phone Shirley says, Well, we were all poor then. We didn't know we were. Everyone was.

Georgie's family worked for Muriel's dad. Georgie and Shirley tell stories of walking through the fields. Georgie was the artist among them.

We'd draw pictures and sketch those foundations. I was thirteen, Shirley says. It was 1953 when I moved to the valley. We were about to be flooded out by the reservoir. And back then even, those foundations looked a hundred years old to us.

Hank's cryptic answer is no answer, not for me, not yet: these patroons, rent, a war . . . I stare at their wedding announcement in the local paper for which I now write. It is August 20, 1964; Muriel has just turned twenty-four. In the photo her dress has a scoop collar. Hank and Muriel are both in white; she has pearls at her neck. Articles in the paper say in 1940 a daughter was born. No name is listed, but it's Muriel, the only child. 1946: Her father builds a "new type laminate rafter barn." He takes prizes at the county fair for best Ayrshire cow in 1947. In 1949 his neighbors hold a haying bee when he crushes his hand with a haying fork. And, the wedding: "a floor-length dress, white organza applique lace seed pearls, a fingertip veil of silk illusion and a pill box hat."

—

David is on the phone. He says, She has two kids. We can't—

I don't hear the other side of the conversation. It is 7 p.m. in the UK, and he is talking to his business partner. There would be no one else in the office. I picture the space, on the wall the posters they've designed for clients. Anil—he says of their young designer—he's still at home with his parents.

He studies his screen. I study him. I know they are trying to decide whom to fire. They have a staff of three. They are talking about how much they can still pay them, how little David and his partner can get by on, what both owe on mortgages. David says it's okay for him to skip his salary for a couple months. That terrifies me. I have no idea what we will do or how we will get by. I don't tell him I'm alarmed. When he hangs up, I suggest we return and by that I mean for good, to live again in London. David says no, absolutely not.

The local feed store runs an ad with Muriel's father and one of his prize cows. It is February 1951. He only feeds them

Dugan and Taber Milk Mix. The ad reports his yields. He wears a sweater and a cloth cap. He has hooded eyes and smiles at the cow, holding a feed can. Her name is Sun's Ideal and has a "305-day record 2x milking 13,190 lbs of milk, 564 lbs of fat." Must have been a hard life.

Chapter 9

IN THIS TIME OF LOSS—MY father, Muriel, David his company, and my village even more than that—I meet the bottle gentian, a flower that is its own crazy purple, a royal blue so bright I'd like to compare it to something so you can see it. Thoreau tried. He compares it to the male bluebird. That bird, though, is not blue at all, but black. The color is a trick of the light, and this plant has a trick too. It never opens. I return over and over waiting for the bud to bloom, but nothing. The flower stays closed. No one would ever think it's a viable plant. I learn it requires specialized pollinators to force their way in. One drills in at the bottom; another pushes in at the top. All around it the goldenrod has gone gray, and the gentian glows an electric blue so bright it looks lit from within.

This autumn—they are a fall flower, the last of the blooms—I walk through fields and forests with a logger running for office. Because of financial catastrophes that feel like our town's abandonment as well as flooding that does not spare the basement of the house with the turret, I interview all the candidates for the paper. I want to know how each envisions our community's future. He is logging this parcel. He will say he hates politics and tells a story of meeting a politician in Albany who claimed to be a farmer. He tells me the politician "'has on probably an eight, nine-hundred dollar pair of shoes,' and I say, 'You,

you have no I.D.'" He pronounces the word as two letters, I. D. instead of idea. He says to the politician, "'You're supposed to be a farmer and represent farmers. The shoes you're wearing cost more'n most farmers make in a year.'"

I see the dairy farmer at church and his large belt buckle and Wrangler jeans and how he worried at his coffee cup, one corner tearing off as we spoke.

A cluster of gentians appears in a clearing. I show them to the logger. The blue blazes against the fading grass.

He says if he could be a professional hunter he would. Instead here, at least, I get to be in the woods, outside all the time. I tell him the gentians are rare, and he says, I had no I.D.

A year later, David comes in second to him in a logging competition, and I am proud. This lumberjack has been named the top logger for twenty Eastern states. David shrugs off this second place and says it was a distant second. He smells of sweat. He has on a pink shirt and orange Kevlar chaps. We joke about his quitting his job, becoming the pink forester—for both his shirt and his politics. David and his partner have dissolved their business, but he is okay. He is happy with work and will be for a good few years. He serves as a designer for a friend's marketing agency in London. The two talk daily, and their projects are creative and collaborative, making books, exhibitions, and campaigns.

The bottle gentian is closed to outsiders. With frost it goes brown, yet the flower keeps its shape. The petals are always closed to protect its sex, its reproductive organs, from the cold. It is a "species of concern."

I email photos of it to my mom. Gentians are named for Gentius, an Illyrian king who took on Rome and supposedly discovered the plant's roots make a bitter tonic.

———

In New York City and other cities people take to bridges and march in masks. They campaign for the 99 percent. The country is talking about how the rich become richer, and the poor or just the rest of us are not, with healthcare and other cares and demands. The police arrest hundreds of people crossing the Brooklyn Bridge. Those in bandanas and masks are charged with "loitering and wearing a mask" because of a law from 1845.

———

In a year, ads emblazoned with a tea bag appear in the local paper for which I write. One has the tea bag made of stripes and stars. Another time the tea bag is a whole half page asking: How Much Immigration Is Too Much?

———

It is Rudd who first tells me about the Anti-Rent War. He mentions in passing an uprising here on the farms. I read about it next in a giant tome on the Catskills nearly a thousand pages long. Subtitled "From Wilderness to Woodstock," it tucks the story into a few slim chapters in the middle. I learn that Moses Earle subscribes to the *New-York Tribune*, Horace Greeley's newspaper. A few years later Greeley signs up Karl Marx as a correspondent. There is the patroon, too, of Hank's email and these men in their costumes, the Calico Indians. I don't know what the name means, not why it was coined or how. These are all still just discrete facts, none of which links up yet as way to make sense of this place. Rudd later texts me a link to a PDF of a book on the Anti-Rent War written in 1906.

—

In the book, one old-timer says, "If it had happened after the Civil War it would have been a war of blood."

—

In the parade that August, the men twirl in their dresses and mask. They shake toward the crowd and away. David takes my hand, and up the street attention turns to a long table for a watermelon-eating contest. The prize goes to a little girl with pink juices down her face. Her hair is tied back in a braid. David says we should go. Summer is so urgent, pressing and passing so fast. There is much to do and a frost in less than a month.

—

The tea bag ads continue:
+ Your Second Amendment Rights??
+ DC: Take Back Your government.
+ NYC Land, Tax And Our Taxes.
+ Freedom Rights and Responsibilities (Pt II)

—

No one knows for sure why the Calico Indians wear those disguises. One historian, Reeve Huston, ties it to cruel, performative behavior meant to enforce social norms— men in dresses who'd crudely serenade newlyweds with pots and pans and torment those who broke sexual norms. He also points out the sheer maleness of the

Calico Indians, and that most of these men in dresses are young and dispossessed. No-hopers, like punk, I think, born of a recession and flaunting rules. Another account by Harvard historian and Standing Rock Sioux citizen Philip Deloria links it back to just after the English Civil War of the 1660s. Then, people in blackface, Blacks, they were called, would steal—poach—the wealthy landowner's deer. These Blacks are poor, pinched, and pressed; the lines between protesting, clowning, and violence are thin.

This behavior travels in time to the colonies, to the Boston Tea Party where men dress as Mohawks, drawing on that combo of terror and protest but also linking themselves to the Indigenous people here, as if these men in disguise are the country's true citizenry. Just after the Revolution, more white men dressed as "Indians" appear during the Whiskey Rebellion and even in one incident in Upstate New York. Someone calling himself a Native shoots a sheriff trying to enforce a rent sale in 1791.

Whatever the reason exactly and however it comes to the Anti-Renters, the disguises give them the freedom to break the law. Then the law is changed to make the costumes illegal.

—

It is September, not even a month after the parade. The sheriff "swears in" Ozzie, a drug-sniffing dog named after murdered lawman Osman Steele. With his human partner, he makes his first arrest the next day with a traffic stop at 1 a.m.

> In a search of the car, Ozzie found several glassine envelopes of heroin. . . . The use and sale of illegal drugs and prescription narcotics is on the

rise in Delaware County, said undersheriff Craig DuMond, "I'm expecting, based on the level of drug activity we have in the county, that the team will be very busy," DuMond said. "You're going to see a lot of them out there."

The dog, K-9 Ozzie, costs the county nothing. He is supported entirely with volunteer donations.

—

In the recession more people go to graduate school because there is little work. School fees rise; students take on more debt. More people are trained for academic jobs, and universities cut those jobs replacing them with part-time teaching positions that have no benefits. They come instead with titles like "instructor," "lecturer," or "adjunct," sometimes "associate." I become one of the adjuncts. At NYU I teach contemporary art and theory. I joke that I am a Walmart worker of education, because how else to explain it? Soon articles start running every six months or so about adjuncts on welfare, living in their cars, struggling to teach and make ends meet.

I look out at the lecture hall filled with fifty students: the three girls, silent, skin pale as skim milk who always sit in the middle, four boys studying engineering, another woman doing early childhood ed., one person who dresses like I did in the early nineties—cropped top and high-waisted black jeans. She always arrives late and tries to close the heavy doors as quietly as possible. There's another woman from Texas in a pink hijab. The first day after class she approaches the front of the room and stands at the end of a line of students with questions. She says she is nervous and knows nothing of art. I tell her it's okay, that no one in this room does. I want to add, me included. Before each class, I feel dizzy and unprepared, so I overprepare.

The class is called Art of Now, with bombast in its name, and is only supposed to cover the last ten years, but I use history and talk of photography and Sojourner Truth and Frederick Douglass. Standing in the classroom with its sloped seating like a cinema, I think of all the forces that have brought us to this moment, a recession and my fear of not being whatever-enough to teach, and my students' loans, and this school, one of the wealthiest private landlords in New York City, and how the university gives almost no money in financial aid. Here in this room I am earning about what my neighbors do a hundred-and-some miles away for a job that gives me a title and seeming status, and my students are either rich or in debt, and the school itself owns properties across Lower Manhattan and into Brooklyn, none of which the university pays tax on. Facing out at the room as the projector hums, I think that the school is a real estate scam; yet I love teaching and being here with the students and their willingness to open themselves up to art that looks strange and unfamiliar, and I think of all that ties us together.

Over the semester the woman from Texas emails me about feminism and race and sexualization and representation. She will go on to get a PhD and work in prisons with those who have converted to Islam.

In the uprising the men are "laborers." They have no future, they are land-poor, resource deprived, and at this point in time they are also hungry.

In the picture, my parents kiss and there is joy. It is inescapable, and then it is Upstate New York and that wave in my mom's hair. There is Squeaky the cat and the American Gothic photo. Then they move to Washington and their worlds divide. My father works on co-operatives; my mom looks after the home and kids. Each cedes the other's realm. She is an economist in an entire subdivision of economists, it seems; other women with the same degrees and dreams. It is also full of cooperatives for the trash, water, and babysitting, even the preschool, as if to show how much these women value shared labor and struggle. In my parents' marriage tectonic plates split and separate, drifting apart. By the time I come along there are set lines, battles over toast that conceal so much unsaid, so much my mother will not say, so toast and the degree to which it is charred becomes the subject. Growing up, I become my mom's adjunct in these arguments. My father travels, and she is home alone with me. On long walks up dirt roads, she takes my hand. I hear too much about their relationship and her loneliness and begin to take her side. I am nothing if not my mother's child.

—

On Muriel's father's fields and the lane to nowhere, single-file dog tracks cross our path in the snow. They belong to a coyote, we realize. The heat from its paws makes impressions in the surface. You can count each pad and see the deep imprint of its four claws. Others are here too—rabbits, mink, and deer. Their hoofs leave quotation marks as if they are talking. All the animals are, and it's clear we are not alone no matter how empty the land seems. It's shared with people as well, their lives held in the lines of stone walls. Everything is so still, the air so quiet; there's the held breath and elation as we trespass on their terrain.

In the distance the tips of the boughs are red as if to declare even today, even in December, even at -1, they are reaching for spring.

—

In spring and summer, whenever I go to the waterfall, sunlight overhead casts a verdant glow through the grass and trees. In late autumn, the spray outlines the hill in rime. The falls hold geologic time. Cut steep in the ravine, I'm sure they will, over millennia, grow into a canyon. Over time too there's what I learn of Steve and Rudd, the missing third of Rudd's finger from a logging accident that he shrugs off, and Steve's glee as he talks of mowing fields, or forestry, or raising chickens, or growing and selling potatoes when he was little and what he's convinced is our "potato terroir," as he calls it, giving the word a French spin through the chalky sound of his voice. I will learn that in high school Rudd's teachers called him Bumppo, for Natty Bumppo, as if my friend with his thinning hair and wool hats were some trapper from a James Fenimore Cooper novel, never lost no matter how far he wanders. There are stories people tell of how when he was a teenager he crawled into a cave after a bear. I ask him if it's true and he says yes. I learn how people see him as synonymous with this place, as if he is the place itself.

—

The land itself holds time. Walking up Pakatakan, at first we just see a trail up a low mountain, pleased we have a place to hike in the Catskill Park without ever needing to get into a car. We find a wooden desk there, just off the path. Its seat and table are built at odd heights no one would use for writing. We joke that I will come here to write. I never do. The desk sits on a small spit of private land that's posted. Over the years I learn the desk is for shooting. The wood splinters and rots. The top gets covered in moss and graffiti. There is another spot on the slope near a marked spring where we will find black trumpet mushrooms one year the day before a flood. Just up the hill is a downed tree where we will pick another fungus, chicken of the woods, on David's birthday, and this "will" denotes a future tense more than a decade away. Those places always mark the flood and the birthday and memory.

One autumn near the summit, the oak leaves are thick and slippery. I study the ground with each step and find low black spikes growing from an oak's roots. The spikes appear from the leaf litter and spiral up like pine cones. I assume it's some kind of moss, but it is actually a flower gone to seed, called bear corn. It doesn't have leaves and can't photosynthesize; it depends on the tree roots for its nutrients. The only parts of the plant that appear are these spires, and they depend on the bears and mice and squirrels eating the seeds to spread. And, each time I descend Pakatakan I will remember my first winter floating on pillows of snow in a blizzard. All these times are held at once, no longer then and then and then but simultaneous. They are here, now—us united across time.

Along the roads, I see the saffron-orange salamanders, and eventually there will be ash trees marked with orange blazes. The salamanders are efts, the adolescent form of the eastern newt. Normally the eft lives in damp woods, but it's got a proclivity for pavement in the rain, and I will take to the streets to rescue these wanderers. The efts breathe through their skin and are magic for a million reasons. They're gape-mouthed, meaning an eft can eat something as big as it is, and it can regenerate limbs and its eyes—even, I read, its heart. The eft is special, though, because it holds place and time in its body. The first damp night of spring it always returns to its home pond.

Over the years—years so far in the future at this point—orange spray paint appears on the scabbed bark of trees. The bark peels off, revealing the flesh beneath gone hard and dark. These trees are white ash, and those marks are because of borers. The borers are emerald-green insects killing the trees. The orange blazes are death marked out where road crews will fell the trees, and these trees hold time, living two hundred years or more, and they will come to disappear in my time here.

—

An editor emails asking for more and more backstory in the crime novel. Soon the backstory subsumes the story, and the writing gets shouldered out as I try to answer her queries about how all these elements connect and explain the characters' motivations. I can't simply say this is how it seems, but have to show how it comes to be, and I get caught in the details. They take over the page. Instead I stare at the quotes on the wall and rearrange them as if their relationship to each other is enough. Maybe even these quotes might speak for me—or of my process and my quest.

—

As I write, all time starts to exist together, and chronology collapses as a structure. Time becomes porous and alive. Connections come from proximity. I read another writer, Yiyun Li, talk about time. She says that in Chinese, her native language, verbs don't come with tenses, with past, present, or futures. Instead "context," she explains, carries this sense. In Margaretville we live on the edge of the Devonian Sea and its floodplains. A fossilized tree some twenty-six feet high is found under a dam for one of the city's reservoirs. The city lends the tree and its fossils to the town. This is my context.

The trees pull enough carbon from the atmosphere to support life on earth. It is 385 million years ago:

> This was also a significant moment in the history of the planet. The rise of the forests removed a lot of Carbon Dioxide from the atmosphere. This caused temperatures to drop and the planet became very similar to its present-day condition.

Part II

THE EIGHTH MOON

Chapter 10

IN THE SUNROOM THAT LOOKS over the mountain, there is a white sky and gray snow. It is a winter of storms with names—one called Jonas and a takeover of a wildlife refuge called Malheur. Like bad spirits rising.

There is a blood moon. We huddle in a field just outside the tent. We're wrapped in blankets, the ground below us hard and frozen. This moon comes with prophecies. Two Christian pastors make the news saying this eclipse is a portent of tumultuous times. On his phone David tries to capture the moon. It turns red and bloody as if it has disappeared behind the sun. The photos don't come out. The bloodied orb is impossible to see.

My mother starts hospice. In the hospital a machine beeps as it monitors her breath and heartbeat. Every edge in the room is curved plastic, like a toddler's toy: the machine on wheels with the beeps and lights; the rails on the side of her bed; the tray table, its edges fat and exaggerated as if to say they are friendly and unthreatening, no danger to anyone at all as my mom is trapped and tracked in her bed.

It's nearly noon. She sleeps. I refresh the *New York Times* homepage over and over. Two men press their cheeks together in front of the Supreme Court; a young woman is arrested for scaling a flagpole and tearing down the Confederate Flag; funerals are held in Charleston; Greece has shut its banks. A nurse takes my mother's temperature. A white board says: Today is . . . the weather is . . . your tech is . . . your nurse is . . . your temperature is . . . Beneath that underlined twice is FALL RISK.

The nurse writes 100.3 in blue marker. My mom looks over. "How long have you been here?"

Not long, I lie.

Outside thick, humid haze presses on the horizon. She asks about my drive, tells me she's okay, tired.

I ate all of my breakfast, she says brightly. I note the applesauce stockpiled in round plastic containers, mirroring the rounded edges of her rolling table.

An hour later I slide into her bed next to her. She is so skinny we both fit. My laptop is propped open on the table. It's just after the summer solstice. We watch Obama's eulogy in Charleston.

Onscreen the president talks of greater justice. He believes, he says, that there are better days off in the distance. Poverty, mission, ministry, he repeats.

My mother holds my hand. Her skin is wrinkled, the veins bright blue. Dull splotches dot her knuckles. Her nails are thick, yellowing. The walls in the room are lemon yellow, and she is in a dusty-blue hospital gown with red socks, coded for her chance of tripping should she get out of bed without help. The president says that to put faith in action is more than individual salvation—to feed the hungry, clothe the naked . . . house the homeless . . . This church represents human dignity and human rights. For every American who cares about the steady expansion of human rights and human dignity, in this country, for a foundation of liberty and justice for all. His voice lifts. The clergy behind him rise, and purple satin vestments wave in the TV lights. Applause soars.

Yesterday the doctors said she has a few weeks. Today they decide she has pneumonia. It is as if she's dying of the same things that killed my father, and some of the internists will insist it is cancer.

See that; a man in a lab coat will point this afternoon to a dot on an image of my mother's lung. Another will just mention the dot's size, and I will insist we discuss her dehydration, nausea, and vomiting. My voice will rise. My mother will refuse a CT scan.

What is the point? she says. If it's the cancer, I'm not going to treat it. Not at this age, not after all this time.

The president talks of grace. He's been reflecting on it this week. I don't look at her. I stare at the screen. She runs her finger over my hand, stroking it like she did when I was little. I feel the dry tips of her fingers on my skin for years after. I want to believe there are better things ahead, things my parents fought for—civil rights and voting rights and equal rights. The president intones how sweet the sound that saved a wretch like me.

On the phone my older sisters and I conference about my mom's care. The president says God's grace is there for all of us. We are all sinners. The tech comes in and says he'll come back. The president talks of what we might do with this grace, this chance to see how scarred our country was, that we can still work to be a more perfect union.

In the eternal present of my mind as I type this. I think of time flattening, progress, perfection, perfectability. The myths upon which we, we my family, and we a country, are based.

The camera pans out to the crowd, all in black, but for the dead pastor's two young daughters. They are children.

They wear pink and white dresses and white ankle socks. The president talks of criminal justice reform. He says whatever solutions we find will be incomplete.

On our land the beaver dam breaks. The beavers, those socialists, have abandoned their lodge and moved upstream. With the freezing and thawing and snow and ice expanding and contracting and pressing on the sticks and mud the beavers so diligently laid up, the dam can't hold—not any longer.

A wall of water rises. It rushes down the stream and past our house through the village. The volunteer fire department is called out to investigate. The water will make its way to the city. The water is a substance of two places. Rising, uprising.

In the hospital on-screen the president sings the chorus of an abolitionist hymn. My mother still holds my hand. Afterward, after I am crying and the lid is down on my computer, she pronounces the speech, "Too Christian, too churchy. Why did he have to do that?"

This could be funny or it could be her humor in this moment, but she has cancer, or pneumonia or both, like my dad, and we have watched a eulogy, and now the president is too religious.

Grace? she says, That's not going to save us. And, God? Hasn't religion done enough already?

It is spring again. Her death comes in the season called mud. It's also a season of fires, brush fires. There are burn bans, because all the fallen leaves and dead grass can ignite spontaneously. The only things green outside are moss and lichen. Their viridescent brilliance bewilders me. One grows in rough, etched circles and looks heraldic. I try to take a rubbing of the heraldic lichen. I want to capture all of its exquisite beauty. I want to run my fingers over the grooves and patterns in the cool rock, as if they could tell me about her life.

—

On the mountain Pakatakan, ephemerals appear. They are the first flowers of this season of mud and fire. The blooms are fleeting, here and gone: bloodroots with their dark-red sap. A single leaf and flower unfurl together. Spring beauties swirl pink and white like a starlight mint and bleeding hearts feel as my heart. They are pale yellow. Another is dusty purple yet its name is blue, blue cohosh. The leaves point up at any small sliver of light and look like a crone's hand, knotted with arthritis, reaching for the sky.

—

As she is dying, her hands too grasp at the air, for invisible cobwebs spinning above. Sometimes she touches her forehead, in pain it looks like. I want her to put her arm down. I hold her left hand and tell her I am here and not going to leave.

—

In the sachem Cacawalemin's woods I see my mother walk slowly and greet every bloom.

—

The lichen rubbings fail. All that shows up are gray scratches on paper, and the paper goes into my pocket and now is on my desk.

One kind of moss is not really a moss at all. It looks like miniature evergreens clinging to the soil. It's called a club moss and is considered a living fossil, as if it captures ancient time itself. They too helped change the atmosphere, and here they are at my feet on the forest floor.

—

Meanwhile a year before, we began building a version of my parents' house on Muriel's land. Like Steve and Jane's, it's a recreation, and I want to plant my parents' values here, to make this my foundation in this place, with the kin and ship. Right now, though, the home looks like a UFO has landed in the field. The week of my mom's memorial service the builder quits, leaving debts we cannot cover, and had my mother not died, we would have lost the land and the half-built house. The outside of the structure is covered in shiny metal insulation. It gleams in the light like a dare.

Chapter 11

RUDD STANDS BY THE COLLAPSED beaver dam with David and me. He walks to the berm that had been a dam, that is now covered in brush. The spired tops of old meadowsweet poke up. I am silent and study the desiccated blooms. They look like tiny beads, and there are Rudd's boots—the rubber and leather—and David's face—the colors in his beard—and Rudd speaks. I don't hear what he says but the crunch of his and David's feet on the dead grass. I watch their actions as if they belong to people I don't know, people who stand at a far remove from me, as if I am on a distant shore. My chest is tight, and in grief I am in two places at once, here and not here; here and on that distant shore, separated by a gulf of deep black water. Rudd says something about the beavers and David some thing else, and somehow I am speaking. A voice emerges. I say, There's this shed up the hill.

Now their two faces are trained on mine. David says, Jen? Rudd: A shed? Is it wet up there? So, how big is it?

David gives some answer about the size, six feet, eight feet, and I hear something about no wider than my shoulders. He says some words about crooked steps, and I realize he means the doorway. I hadn't meant to change the subject but I can't stop thinking about those stones and walls.

That is no springhouse, Rudd says. It is the house.

He explains that they—whoever they were—built on top of the spring, so inside would be cool to preserve food in summer and winter, like a refrigerator. The water kept food from freezing or spoiling and regulated the temperature, like geothermal in the home. If you can call that place a home.

—

As the place we are building is stalled, all I think about is this other house. Imagine into the lives lived there: the rocks coated by damp moss, the touch-me-nots that grow but never bloom because there's too much shade. The rocks from the foundation have fallen in on themselves and the precarious stone stairs lurch inside. Compared to the barn twenty feet away with its majestic foundation set into the hill, this house is thrown together, and you can see exactly what its occupants valued and prioritized. The livestock, those few cows and pigs Hank mentioned, get the palatial barn with boulders as big as me. Still, I can't even picture life in this shed that is a shack, that was a home for someone.

—

I start to court other spirits, these rocks, those stones, those foundations.

—

David's work begins to change. The company now creates something called "content" for multinationals that produce skin cream and soap, sunglasses and sporting goods. This content lives online in a post that lasts for seconds and disappears. All that labor, he says, months of revisions and focus groups? And maybe someone "likes" it?

I abandon the crime novel but need to go on research-
ing the land. It snows in May and will be the hottest year
on record. Again. On the rhododendron outside a chicka-
dee scolds. On Twitter a blue bird repeats rage red and
roiling. In June a kingfisher lands outside the kitchen of the
queenly home. The kingfisher's scientific name comes from
"halcyon." In ancient Greece, legend has it, the god of the
winds protected the kingfisher's nest in winter. Those two
weeks free from storms are the halcyon days. Meanwhile,
politicians are promising a return to a past America that
was great. I keep picturing the bear dragging itself through
the woods and the miles it walked. David brought the skull
home, and it sits in the dining room.

In Margaretville, pocket constitutions are given out
at stores. This kingfisher, this halcyon bird, is named for
Alcyone, the daughter of Ceyx, the god of winds. She
marries the son of the North Star. He dies in a storm at
sea and the gods take pity on her grief, turning them both
into birds. The daughter of the winds is perched in a tree
outside, and her call sounds like a metallic rattle, a warning rasped to keep away. Our neighbors paint a sign for a
candidate who courts racists.

It is a summer of alarm. The siren circles. Anger grows.
Here the Confederate flag makes national news when the
county fair refuses to ban it.

David teaches me the acronym of assistance and care as
we fell trees for our firewood. He shows me the hinge plan
and the escape plan, these two Ps that go with the initials,
the HELPP.

Measure the tree, he says. Your hinge should be—he
draws his finger across the maple's girth—80 percent of

the diameter at breast height. His breast and mine are at different heights. He tells me, Don't forget the back-cut plan, thickness no more than 10 percent of your diameter. He lines up the tree with the saw. I kneel behind him to see his angle. He says, So it will land where you aim. He looks in the distance. I am too scared to down the tree. I cut a scrappy hawthorn near the shack that was a shed, and afterward I have a thorn stuck in my side. I have go to the doctor to get it removed. It costs $300 for two inches of thorn, which can harbor an array of pathogens.

———

Anger, I read, makes pain more intense, and harder to treat. Alleviating it requires more pain medicine, more opioids, but chronic pain also causes anger. Anger helps people feel in control.

———

I go out for long walks because they help with my grief, because in walking I talk to my parents. Grief is strange; time blurs. The dead are alive and present. On the ground those miniature fir trees, the club mosses, are impossibly small, smaller than a seedling. It takes them twenty years to spore and come to sexual maturity, a time frame like a human's. They are what remain of the first plants on earth. Here walking with the dead, the years, the fossils, the moss, the selves, we are all together in time. I feel too all the other people on the land beating and breathing into this moment with me. And, because my parents are gone and Muriel is gone, I search for connections where maybe none exist. I delve into that shack that was a shed, and its trash. I pore through my parents' things, look at the photos, wonder at the time of their love and how it fell apart. I study that picture taken in winter outside the co-op. My father looks like a movie star, that grin and the wave in his hair.

I find one speech of his from 1972, where he talks about fair prices for farm products and the cost of out-migration in small rural towns. In another at the dawn of the Reagan eighties, he says that individualism is a problem. "We need," he says, "a new age of commitment."

———

David gets quieter and quieter. His work weighs on him.

———

It is my first day back teaching that fall; I drive the route I always take to the train, through the Hudson Valley town where Sojourner Truth was enslaved and then escaped. She walks, doesn't run, to freedom. She insists on the walking. To run is to do something illegal. It is undignified. Now a statue of her as a young girl stands on a sidewalk by the only stoplight in town. She and her family were owned by Col. Johannis Hardenbergh. He fought in the Revolution. His father is the Hardenbergh of the patent, and his name is still on our deed.

———

A HILLARY FOR PRISON sign is stuck in the embankment just above the flashing stoplight that serves as the entrance to my village.

———

I ask the head of the local historical society about the shed that is a house, and she emails a map from 1869. Called a

Beers map for its publisher, the image looks vaguely familiar. Two maps, two times, this time. The roads hew to ones I know even if the names are different—and the names are tantalizing: Sunny Dale, Reserve Home, Union Home, Quiet Reserve, Silver Dale, Solitude. So many dales, homes, and reserves, as if to speak of some pastoral fantasy. Over Solitude in tiny letters: "INSANE RETREAT."

I trace my finger through Margaretville and up onto Bull Run. A double line appears where the lane, our land, should be. Where Muriel once picked blackberries, where the stone ruins stand.

———

It is early fall; David and I pick the blackberries and make jam. One neighbor warns of a bear. I am not sure it's a real danger. Still I exhort David to keep speaking as we pick to keep the bear at bay. It's just a way to get him talking.

In the tent we keep a bear whistle.

On the Beers map this line for our land doesn't go anywhere or link to anything. It just dead-ends near the tent. Next to it is a name: J Clum. Where Muriel's house stands is "A Kettle SUNNY SIDE." And each name has a number: 128 for Clum, 127 for Kettle. The numbers are consecutive, but I have no idea what they mean, maybe simply that the people are neighbors?

The election looms. I talk to my parents in the plants and sweep the leaves from the floor. I read again the lines about the individual and all this I, I, I, in "the age of self-fulfillment," my father called it. All this I, he said, was damaging, "where many individuals, too many, are asking questions like how can I satisfy all my needs and desires; how much commitment should I make when I have other things I want to do even more? What does personal success really mean in terms of what one must sacrifice?"

(I think about moving everything to the present tense.)

Soon a president-elect is praising the forgotten men and women of America, and the news people are talking about the shock of our lives, how the earth moved under our feet. There is this versus that, urban versus rural, young versus old, rich versus poor, but the poor are siding with the rich, the men against the women, the whites against everyone else. In the rust belt, the belt has tightened. Hate is state sponsored. There are colors: blue, red, and purple, and on the land all is the shade of dun and dust—the dead grass and my deadened heart and the goldenrod that has gone gray, and the dead and dying pines at the edge of the beaver pond where the beavers flooded the trees' root systems. Rudd tells me he voted for the Green Party candidate.

And, the gentian's electric shade of violet remains.

———

Two days after the election I'm in the city to teach. I talk about history and protest, ACT UP and die-ins, people throwing loved one's ashes over the White House fence. I quote Sojourner Truth, "I sell the shadow to support the substance." She who'd do whatever she could to support abolition, whose first language was Dutch, who still could not read or write, who gave speeches and sermons, who was the first Black person to sue for her child to be freed from slavery after he has been stolen from her, sits with her sewing in this photo looking stately. It is adorned with this legend on the screen before me. The shadow here, her image, herself. And, I say to the class, if she could fight, I certainly can. I'm standing at the front of a proscenium arch and search the fifty faces before me. I ask what they think. I swallow, look down. My throat tightens. Silence fills the lecture hall. I wear a mic so they can hear me, and I wonder if they hear my breath.

Someone sets a coffee cup down; a jacket rustles. More sounds of weight shifting, someone coughing, time elapsing. The projector hums. Dust motes catch in the light. A student raises a hand and asks about violence. "I get protest, but what about violence? What would you do? Where do you draw the line?"

Chapter 12

IT IS EARLY SPRING, ANOTHER year, an earlier year, after we find the hunting blind and before the bear dies and the Constitution is passed out in stores. I stand in a field. As much as "hollow point" sounds like a landmass, an aching place of desolation and loneliness overlooking some body of water, I mean the bullet. It is snub-tipped and stamped "Winchester" at the base. A pile of them lies in a plastic bag at my feet. I am learning to fire a gun to write the crime novel that connects too much. In it I cannot see what to leave out in order to tell the story, the plot. In it a body is found on New York City land. In it there is the elusive hunting blind. PJ and Silent James discover the body, and Steve and Jane's daughter, the hydrologist, is now a city water cop, a detective. In the manuscript she is also still a hydrologist, but this information is too much to explain here, too much about New York City water politics and civil service pay grades.

An actual water cop for the city teaches me to shoot. He lives upstate and is police for water, for the water that is here and there, for fears of terrorism and water supplies, but often just to keep people from swimming in the city's reservoirs. He's also told me about the domestic disputes he's had to go to and dealing with schizophrenic people off their meds, here in a county the size of a state where there is little mental health coverage. We stand in the field by the tent at dusk. There is no green, little grass. Birds sing evensong. The sun glints in one chink of steel slate sky.

I hold my friend the cop's Glock. It feels like a toy, so much of it is plastic.

He shows me the rifling inside the chamber. He asks if I ever read the Chomsky interview the IWW published. My friend the cop has broad, wide shoulders, a stubness like the bullet but also a squareness, as if compressed into a frame. He is a runner and served as an Army Ranger and has a degree in anthropology. He says, I'll send it to you, the Chomsky.

The bullet is a physics lesson. Copper is a soft metal, which means it is more deadly. It will splay on impact to do the maximum damage. He tells me about the bullets and their power and how he hates his job. He is thinking of leaving to become a social worker.

Afterward he hands me a single bullet to take home. It sits on the kitchen sill. He tells me to wash my hands after touching it. Bullets have heavy metals, he says—and gunpowder, you don't want to be eating that or get it in your eye. He is a gentle teacher.

Now as I write, I roll the bullet in my palm to conjure that moment, and I do not wash my hands but continue typing.

The soothing things he says about the gun:

+ "For the trigger, squeeze it softly, tenderly." It sounds sweet, the way he puts it.
+ "Tenderly," he says again, "the shot should surprise you; your touch is so gentle."
+ "And the breath, your breath, your body relaxes on the exhale. That is when you squeeze. You cup the

gun"—he takes my hands—"this is how you hold it." He fits the soft fleshy pads of my palms together around the handle.

+ "Marry them," he says.

I have the gun and don't put my eye to it, as he has told me. I close my left eye, and from my right I spot the target and squeeze gently, softly.

In the now of writing I tape that Chomsky quote to the wall next to Adrienne Rich:

> If you look at those people and listen to them on talk radio, these are people with real grievances. I listen to talk radio a lot and it's kind of interesting. If you can sort of suspend your knowledge of the world and just enter into the world of the people who are calling in, you can understand them. I've never seen a study, but my sense is that these are people who feel really aggrieved. These people think, "I've done everything right all my life, I'm a god-fearing Christian, I'm white, I'm male, I've worked hard, and I carry a gun. I do everything I'm supposed to do. And I'm getting shafted." And in fact they are getting shafted. For 30 years their wages have stagnated or declined, the social conditions have worsened . . . there's nothing, so somebody must be doing something to them, and they want to know who it is. Well Rush Limbaugh has answered—it's the rich liberals who own the banks and run the

government, and of course run the media, and they don't care about you—they just want to give everything away to illegal immigrants and gays and communists and so on.

Well, you know, the reaction we should be having to them is not ridicule, but rather self-criticism. Why aren't we organizing them?

—

The gun is mentioned in Elizabeth Hardwick's opening. It's been hanging here on the wall. I have history and the smell of gunpowder, sweet and acidic, its tang at the back of my throat. The sound echoes against the opposite ridge and trees.

—

I am in a municipal building in a town called Delhi, pronounced del-high. The county seat, it's named for the branch of the Delaware River that runs through it, and the river is named for the British colonizer Baron De La Warr. His name has also been foisted on the Lenape nations whose lands stretch out around the river across several states, including here.

In the county clerk's office on the third floor, florescent lights hum overhead. I'm looking up deeds. It turns out those numbers on the map I was sent, that 128 next to Clum and the 127 by Kettle, are plots of land in the Hardenbergh Patent. A handful of people in dad jeans and white sneakers hover around two monitors on their phones. The room is lined with bookcases full of titles and deeds. The indexes alone are so unwieldy they sit on rollers so you can pull them out. One of the hovering people reads out three numbers into his phone. "Umm hmm," he says in response to whoever is on the line.

I search pages of grantors and grantees, years and dates. The books include a cross-listing for something called a liber, and I have no idea what that means. I ask a woman operating a copy machine. A sign above her says, THE USE OF *ANY* CAMERA IS STRICTLY PROHIBITED.

The air has the chemical smell of copier ink, the kind of thing that in London would have made me sick. I stifle a cough. The clerk doesn't glance up from the giant volume before her. She says, It's *book* in Latin.

I feel stupid for not knowing.

The deeds are written in fountain pen with fancy flourishes nearly impossible to decipher, and the words seem to be in a foreign language. The sentences are knotted with strange phrases that repeat in each document: "appurtenance" and "indenture," "situate" instead of "situated." Each deed references "heirs and assigns," and "assign" I realize is not a verb but a noun, a person. These two, "the heirs and assigns" mean whoever will inherit the land in the future. It's a phrase to designate forever and ever. This is the language of capitalism, of ownership. There is also "quiet and peaceable possession." I find that in liber 56 describing lot number 128.

That is my lot, my land. It's 1862. Morgan Lewis's grandson and his wife, Robert J. and Louisa Livingston, sell to someone who owns a dry goods store in Margaretville. Liber 56 records: "The Livingstons of New Brunswick in the state of New Jersey, sell and witnesseth . . . all that juice [later, I tease out that it's a lowercase *p* that looks like a *j*; the word is "piece"] or parcel of land situate in the said town of Middletown." Reading through the thickets of language I learn Morgan Lewis originally leased the lot to a Peter Klum on the thirteenth of December 1841.

These are the Livingstons of Livingston Manor, all three Livingston Manors, the one in the Hudson Valley, another in the Catskills, and the third in New Jersey, whose family members sign the Declaration of Independence and the Constitution. Morgan Lewis: owns my town, starts NYU where students pay $75k a year to attend and incur $200k or more in debt by the time they graduate. And, most professors like me are adjuncts with pay that is not a living, that asks us either to be born of privilege or live with privation. Either way, in our wages is an assumption of work that might be a calling, and assumptions of students' lives with debt.

In the deed, I find that Louisa Livingston is made to sit an examination with the commissioner of deeds. He questions her separately from her husband to make sure she agrees with the sale, and the language is clinical:

"The said Louisa M on a private examination by me apart from her husband acknowledged that she executed [I think that's the word] the same freely and without any fear or compulsion of her said husband."

Picture the scene, a woman of great wealth in the drawing room of her Greek revival mansion, her second home. She lives mostly in New York City, but here she is visited by a man in a dark suit and has to swear that she agrees to the sale, and maybe I'm grateful that a woman's agreement isn't taken for granted by dint of simply being married. There is also a strange medical feeling in being "examined" alone.

Around me the snatches of conversations are whispered into phones, as if the people are speaking to the air.

"Examine," I think of being examined under these bright lights of the clerk's office. Here in this building with its mansard roof and municipal-yellow paint, zoom in on the people in their white sneakers and scuffed shoes and bags splayed on the tops of bookcases. A woman clutches her phone with her shoulder. Someone in a pink pilled sweatshirt says, "Can you ask again for numbers, deed number. And the seller?" Words swell and circle. A man talks to the shelves as if to shield his words: "You can tell the bank, I'll send the deed info now." I realize these are people doing title searches for banks, for mortgages. This is money.

Now telescope out like some long shot in a movie, and from such a distance you will see this character, me, in this room. I have told my students to look to history, and here I am looking at pieces of paper from the 1800s I can barely comprehend. I have no idea what I am doing or digging for, not really. It seems ridiculous in this moment where we've elected a ridiculous president, and my students are scared and my neighbors still have signs up with that new president's name, and I have been so scared of my neighbors' reactions that I woke at 3 a.m. the morning after the election to rip down my own yard signs supporting the other candidate. And, maybe there is no sense to be made. Or maybe this makes as much sense as any, as a way to deal with multiple griefs—familial and national. If I were a character, this would all be knit into story, but here for me in this moment, this pull of the past holds little logic; not to me, at least, not yet.

—

At home going through census records online, I find a Peter Clumb in my township in 1840. Peter Clum without a *B* dies in 1849 of consumption after being sick for ninety days. Others on the same page die of fits, rattles, and giving birth. An *X* is placed in the column where the woman's profession should appear.

The next year Peter Clum's wife Jane is listed in the federal census as the head of the household. She lives with four others: John and Abigail who are in their early twenties; there is eighteen-year-old Catherine and a two-year-old baby girl, also named Jane. Staring at the page and the enumerator's careful penmanship, I realize John is married to Abigail. The two year-old is their daughter, and Catherine is John's sister. I see the dank, damp rocks and foundation with its spring in the middle, and Peter with TB living and dying with all those people around—his son and son's wife and their baby, as well as his own wife and daughter. Jane dies in 1855, and John Clum becomes head of the household. "Farmer" is his title.

—

I realize that one of the people in the county clerk's office, the woman in a caramel-colored turtleneck, also works at the Margaretville thrift store.

—

Seasons pass. Sun. Rain. Rain and snow. Snow. Mud then sun. The greening of grass each day, from the shade of dead stalks to a lemon-bright chartreuse. I look several times a day, and each time I'm sure the color has changed. It is a trick of the light or a trick of time. A snake skitters across the ground on an afternoon that seems too warm for April. Spring comes, with peepers and sex and the drumming grouse, and putting up the tent that is permeable to the world near the foundations. David jokes about the tom turkey whose head goes from red and blue to white for sex when the bird is excited. He says that the turkey is horny and patriotic, and maybe that was how it nearly became the national bird. Turkeys look more like dinosaurs than any other bird I've seen. We wonder if a T-Rex changed colors like that.

A hummingbird flies into the house, attracted to the red flowers on the crown of thorns because nothing outside is blooming yet. We rescue this tiny bird with its iridescent green feathers in a pink ball cap from my parents' co-op. The bird clutches the rim, calmed by being bathed in pink. Outside it sits on the queenly home's porch, stunned. I can see its heart beating, its chest pound. It refuses to leave the hat until I put some sugar water in a red plastic lid. The snake stutters in the dirt. Its movements are incremental, as if it is not sure of enough warmth to slither away from my attention.

I drag David to an old cemetery. It sits on a cross-roads, a shortcut from one two-lane highway to another. He calls out that he's found some Hubbells. And there's a Clum here, he says. Peter Clum's grave says, "aged 48 yrs 2 mos & 16 days." That is all, and that itself is hard to make out for the moss. Jane's children must have erected hers. It says, "She was a loving mother here."

And, here, what? The grass grows green at the edge of her stone from the warmth of the rock. Peter Clum's youngest brother is the first person buried here in 1821.

His headstone is supposed to read: "Here lies Philip Klum who died instantly by the fall of a tree." But we can't find it. We find plenty of other names and dozens of children—graves marked with lambs and names: MALISSA 1854 AGED 4 YRS, 10 MS & 8 DS. The lamb is for someone who dies in youth. Someone else who dies at twenty-two has inscribed at the very bottom of his stone: "This you see as you pass by / As you are now so once was I / As I am now soon you will be / Prepare for death and follow me."

Philip Klum is fifteen. Killed by a tree.

———

On our land are piles of rocks, just heaps of flat stones scabbed with lichen. Called bluestone, they're not blue at all but gray. Looking at the stacks, I'm sure they must mean something. Or, I want them to mean something, to be something, like an ancient burial mound. But they're just where people tossed the boulders they gathered before they could plow the fields, so they could pay their rent in wheat. I picture John Clum and his sister Catherine out collecting them, and before that, Peter girdling trees. You'd cut a circle of bark to kill the tree then burn out the stumps. Before that, the Munsee would have used fire to clear forests and cultivate blueberries and nut trees.

I have moved into a painting, but none of the paintings in the Met show any of this. They're made at the same time but don't bother with the people hauling rock or being killed by a tree. The artists are interested in nature and landscapes, not people—not humans and their struggles. Not the hard life here but what a "wilderness" represented.

The people are so minuscule—if they're shown at all—that they're reduced to the landscape, to something scenic or conquerable. They are nature itself, even though people have been here some seven thousand years or more.

Chapter 13

I FIND A CARBON COPY of a letter my father writes
to Adlai Stevenson just after his defeat in the presiden-
tial election of 1952. My dad is in his early twenties and
says that he is scared of the country and its direction. I am
scared; the world feels unrecognizable, the country even
more so, and I can't imagine feeling close enough to a candidate to write of my feelings or fears. I want to know how
my parents navigated this moment. It is the start of the
Cold War with its witch hunts and the cusp of another war
in Korea, and my father who has served in World War II
writes Stevenson, a left progressive governor who helped
create the UN, that he worries of serving again. The paper
is soft. I read the letter so many times I use up whatever I
can from its words.

At the bottom RIK:lk. Lois has typed it, not Sandy.

A few years before she dies, I'm home sitting with my mom. She is in the easy chair, stacks of books she's reading at her side. The sleeves of her robe puff out like a princess's, and her scrawny legs stick out at the bottom. She wears thick sheepskin slippers though it's summer. Her hair is only flecked with gray. Bobby pins hold it back, and in her I see the ghost of my future, the woman I will one day be, at least in looks, maybe more. I am in her rocking chair.

We drink wine. It is early evening. Light from the setting sun flits through the trees and dapples the room around us. I love the rocker. It's Danish modern—green wool with teak legs that arc into a bow. I sit in it reading every time I am back.

She says, I held you there as a baby. It was the middle of the night, just the two of us the year you were born. She is silent, looks down and back at me. I didn't know, she says, didn't think I could—Martin Luther King had just been killed and then Bobby Kennedy, and I didn't think I could bring a baby into that world. Then there were these hours with you. In the middle of the night you'd be awake, and I would sit there and rock this little baby who was cuddled over my shoulder. We would rock and you would go to sleep. I loved those nights alone together.

I still find the chair a comfort.

———

At the courthouse I find Muriel's deeds, and I think about Thoreau and his miser and the devils, the three stones and the stake. Deeds, though, are like biblical begats—only with capitalism—going back and back and back with owners and history laid out, along with landmarks and anything that can identify a parcel: a stream, a boulder, a cherry tree near a property line. Muriel's also has a name: Augustus Kittle, not Kettle, not like on the 1869 map the town historian sent, or the name of the ridge owned by NYC that it calls Kettle Hill. The name is Kittle.

There are other secrets I can't unravel. Augustus Kittle buys the farm, the same farm, three times over with three different deeds, first in 1847, then 1865, and finally in the 1870s. There is a riddle as well: he doesn't own the waterfall I walked past that first day. Nor did Muriel or her father and grandfather. Each deed specifically excludes the two acres around it. It is strange because the area is marked now with posted signs, and the people who claim it also bought their property from Muriel.

Later I find that Augustus Kittle's firstborn son is named Lincoln. This in 1864 when the Civil War is unpopular in the North. Six months earlier race riots spread across Manhattan and Brooklyn as the draft is imposed in New York. Men are lynched; Black orphanages burned, killing the children inside. Yet on our land a Lincoln is raised. I want proximity and history to connect me to this Augustus and his child.

Then, one more thing: Augustus Kittle is charged with manslaughter in 1845 when he is still a teenager. I have the mystery of three deeds, a name, a murder, and a Lincoln.

———

David and I watch that movie about the Nonpartisan League my parents took me to when I was little. In our living room the dust motes float in the projector's beam. The days are warm. Our windows are open to the night. Outside we hear neighbors out for walks; music flares from pickups. Kids ride by on bicycles. That character me in this book is trying to understand something of my parents and their values. I want to recover their love but also this idea of collectivity that they connected to rural places, my kind of place, a place my father lives almost half his life when not at home with me. I guess, I am in some way working my way back through time to him and my mother, both.

Onscreen a coffin moves across a prairie like in the painting *The Burial at Ornans*, black and heavy, and the sky swallows the bodies. A farm in foreclosure is auctioned. The banker is porcine and loathed. In another shot in a kitchen, people talk about haying, politics, and banks, and how capitalism is killing them all.

Afterward David says, So, you mean your parents made you sit through this? How old were you?

It's beautiful, right. I mean—

He says, But it is half in Norwegian and entirely in black and white, and you were what, six, seven?

It won a prize at Cannes.

I want him to be impressed by my parents' foresight or ambitions, thinking this was an important film to see. I can hear my mom outside the cinema in Washington and can smell the waxy scent of her lipstick, see her skirt and sensible shoes and hear her say that these are the people my dad works with, and my dad will say, Not quite those people. It's their descendants, and she says, Yes, Bob, her voice dismissive. She says that this is the start of rural co-ops, and my dad says, in his work voice that drops down one octave, that the co-ops date back to the 1840s.

Next on the street the two of them are about to argue. Rather, she is about to argue and I am about to take her side, but now here where I slow down on that moment, I hear him say, *movement.* It is the co-op movement, and we are part of it.

———

It is funny; in the present of writing, these things are connected. At the time, in that moment, they weren't, but now where I have cut the interstitials, they are more linked than it would seem at first. Like this: I am in Rudd's "Camp Up North," as he calls it. It's the space over his garage, twenty steps from his front door. It is furnished with a table, an old cook stove, a bed and camp blankets. I'm here to look at his photos, landscapes and shots of nature, details of trees and moss and dew.

He pours green tea from a thermos and wears a faded red shirt. Its collar is frayed and he has a work shirt overtop. He tugs at a button and toys with his mug, looks anywhere, it seems, but at me.

So, this is a studio—what? he asks.

Visit, a studio visit. This is the first time I've seen him nervous.

He has this idea that we should apply for a residency together nearby at Platte Clove, a waterfall that inspired James Fennimore Cooper. He's never done a residency before but suggested that we could do a project together where we pair his photos and my writing. Now I'm going to write our application.

He says, Well, tell me if I do this visit-thing wrong.

I say not to worry and explain what it's like when I do this with other artists. That he can let himself be unknown and exposed feels like a mark of our friendship. He angles his laptop toward me and apologizes—again. He pulls up images from Facebook.

He glances down. You know, I just—I lost—His hard drive died, he says, and the only copies of the photos are here. On-screen, slender saplings are reflected at right angles in water. It's impossible to tell what is real or apparition. Five hundred and fifty-two blue thumbs-up sit beneath it. I say something about how ghostly it appears. He pulls up a picture of a tree, green with lichen. I want to say something about my mom and the rubbing. His tree is surrounded by brush so red the limbs seem to be on fire. Another picture is a single bud encased in ice.

He looks beyond me at the cookstove, at its name, HOME COMFORT in bold letters, as if a comfort to him, and says, The space between the camera and the subject, I think that's part of the picture too, and I believe that whole universe exists between where you're sitting and I'm sitting, and it's considered empty, and to the world that's just empty space.

I love that idea of this space that is empty, that he wants to show me, and that it is full of everything. He studies the laptop. Below the photo are eighty-seven comments and twenty-three shares. Outside I hear a crow, and a dog's bark.

Well, he says, a word to undercut all that empty space, and he jumps up abruptly. Hold on, I got something.

He grabs a crate from a shelf high on the wall. He lays the wooden box before me. It feels secret. I've been in this room countless times, with his complete edition of the collected works of John Burroughs in their leather-tooled bindings and the folding table at which we sit. The air is expectant. He opens the box, and inside a red paisley dress and pantaloons are folded together. A metal horn nestles between them, with a leather mask. It is a disguise from the Anti-Rent War, from the parade in Andes.

Red ribbons and braids dangle in front of the hood. He is laying out something forbidden. This was illegal, he says, and I say I know, even though I don't, not really. I assume the dress must be some replica. He spreads it on the bed. It looks like a housecoat covered in a muddy paisley.

He holds out the mask. It's flat like a deflated football, but with rough slits for the mouth and eyes.

Is it . . . real?

Try it on, Jen. Come on, see what it's like.

I shake my head. Now I am the one with the questions and doubts, and he is himself again: the hazel eyes with their mischief and joy. I say, It's—

It's my great-great-great's, Rudd says.

That's when I realize this is no copy but the actual costume, and it is 180-some years old. I say something dumb about its belonging in a museum, like the New York State Museum. Rudd says, No way is it going somewhere stuck in storage, somewhere like Albany. This is my family, my heritage. Nearly all of the disguises were burned, he says.

But here is one, and he explains how everyone nearby hid out in the valley above his family's farm after the shooting. He pulls the hood on. With its crude holes, he looks like he came out of a horror film. I can just make out his lips and teeth, but his eyes sink in darkness. Eyebrows are roughly sewn on in leather. Stitch marks cross the face. The nose points like a beak, like some hybrid bird-man-monster. Rope threads through the bottom of the hood to tighten it at the throat.

He says, No one could yank it off and expose you.

Reading glasses dangle around his neck, and, this

quotidian symbol of middle age holds him in one world, and the mask makes him part of another.

Rudd tells me he made this box, and here it is in his garage barely protected from the weather and temperature and humidity, and I know this chance may never come again, that he is holding out a secret to me. He says some relative someone named Harvey, wore this disguise. Jen, just put 'er on.

I do. I pick up the mask. There I was playing old-fashioned days when I was little and as a teen wearing black Victorian capes in my goth years—all that dress-up, the LARPing before LARP, and this battle between the before and the here and now. But the now has arrived. It is here in Rudd's garage.

The leather feels like cardboard, stiff in my bare fingers. I pull it over my face. I think about the oils on my nose. I want to say that I see a ghost or a medium, something. I peer through the holes. The leather doesn't smell of anything. The room is unchanged.

Chapter 14

I DREAM OF THE MEN in their masks at the picnic at Moses Earle's farm. Rudd's there too, and their hoods are pushed up and faces exposed. They are told never to reveal themselves, not to anyone outside their tribe, they call it, the eight or ten people who form their cell. Today there's a carelessness, though, danger and daring, damn it all to hell and damn the landlord, no matter the damages.

Then, I see the scene like a photo shoot, this picnic in a field. Golden light gleams through the grasses of late summer. The tablecloth (linen, lace) is spotless. I know the table isn't in a field but hidden by a spring in the woods, and probably no table at all, just a cloth on the ground, muddy now from men who've walked so far. The meal has the feel of the Last Supper. The dishes are all laid out carefully, this food that is so precious, that everyone has been forbidden to eat. Ravenous, they gorge themselves.

Meat and butter, oh, the butter—butter so sweet like clover and honey, that women, wives, and sisters have churned to sell because you need the money, because you need to pay rent. Yet here it is before you, and you gorge on it to spite yourself or maybe because of it. Because pleasure must be seized or stolen.

That meal happens a year after the Anti-Rent War reaches Delaware County.

In the early 1840s, the Anti-Rent campaign spreads across the counties to the north and east, where petitions are signed and sent to the state legislature. There's no violence, not yet. People still hope to change the laws. Finally, in the spring of 1844, the last appeals fail, and the farmers issue a declaration of independence, which is a declaration of war. Just as if this were 1776, they see themselves as finishing the revolution and fighting for freedom from tyranny and outside influence. That spring the protests come home to my county. At first they have the celebratory feel of a party or tent revival. There are parades and picnics with speakers and songs. On the Fourth of July that summer Anti-Rent flags fly and some thousand people turn out. Posters are emblazoned ATTENTION! AWAKE! AROUSE!

People will travel thirty miles to these events. They're held in barns and churches and fields. Signs quoting Leviticus appear in windows and shops. THE LAND IS MINE SAITH THE LORD, the lord here not some lord of the manor but God. All the land belongs to God. Others declare that the EARTH IS FREE. Anti-Rent associations are formed in each town, and dues are collected, two cents an acre, to support the uprising. Those without land pay two pounds, and the proceeds go to pay for court cases challenging landlords' title—and to arm the calico militia.

It is a Tuesday, September third; the war's first skirmishes take place in Roxbury, a few miles north of me. Papers are served to a farmer for delinquent rent. The event is covered in the *New-York Tribune*, where Horace Greeley's newspaper talks about how the Calico Indians "came a-whelping" and lead the deputy who delivers the notice to a field "selected for the ceremony, mounted him on something like an old soap box and served him out with tar and feathers until he was sure he was not himself at all." In October, groups of Anti-Rent associations from across the county meet to choose a slate of candidates for election in November. They call themselves the Equal Rights Party and see these rights as existing broadly, for everyone, everywhere.

———

As I leave Rudd's that afternoon, I tell him he looks terrifying in the mask. Imagine running into you in that in the middle of the night on a road and armed? He says, "Yeah, like ISIS. The Calico Indians were like ISIS."

———

We are in a restaurant now, David, Rudd, and me. I love the camaraderie we all share. Another friend comes to our table; she has ice cubes in her red wine. Bangles clink at her wrist. Her hair is strawberry blond. She teaches in the central school and wears a gossamer blouse. Some bit of dialogue goes here: talking about Rudd's project, building road for the state, or if he will ski that winter; her, about the school and her work in the union and how hard teaching is now with the drug crisis and maybe it is time to retire.

Sometimes with round characters I do not want their flaws to emerge. I want to protect them. Or, myself. I am in the grocery store with David. It is Tuesday, November seventh, and here is our friend, the teacher. Nearly two years ago Rudd enlisted us to support Bernie, and now David, she, and I stand in a long aisle of tea and coffee. David and I have come from the polling station in the town hall. He is searching for Earl Grey tea, for which one seems most like he would get in London. The teacher lifts up packages of green tea: lemon/green? Just green? Mint and green? She clutches several boxes, and I am in a big, chunky sweater an artist friend has knit. Under it is a Nasty Woman T-shirt, not that I love this woman, though a red heart is across my chest. I am eager to have a woman in the White House, and my mother was born not long after women got the right to vote. Because she has died this year, I vote in her stead. All these things happen at once: the tea cartons held aloft by my husband and my friend, and I yank up my sweater to show off the T-shirt, sure we share an allegiance. David says, Well tomorrow this will all be over, and our friend says Hillary is a crook. And, I am too stunned to hear what is said next.

———

The logger who complained about the politician's fancy shoes is quoted in the newspaper pleased with the election, saying, Finally they're paying attention to us. I message him on Facebook saying I hope he's right, that maybe they (an amorphous "they" who are removed from us but suggestive of those in power) will actually support rural America. I am also thinking of my father as I send this note, and how he talked of out-migration and economics and how rural communities get ignored.

———

Come with me now—not this year when the winter is too hot and then too cold. No snow, then snow. Roads close; plows struggle to keep up with a blizzard the news calls "bombogenesis," a neologism that sounds like bomb and genesis, a biblical storm. On screen the radar maps swell with purples, reds, and pinks. Bold letters promise snow falling in inches an hour and drifting across highways with sixty mile-an-hour gusts.

Come back 180 years to those men in dresses and masks. These are young men, some teens, some boys, others in their twenties. It's an age of rage and outrage. Those two words "out" and "rage" do not mean "without rage," because all this anger courses like blood. They blow horns. They amass arms. There is a tin horn nestled next to Rudd's dress. It's usually blown to call men from the fields for lunch. Now it rouses troops.

Is there something more to make clear how this strangeness bends into my life? Reenactment as enchantment, blending into the real as if all IRL? How their rage and mine will run together as a way for me to live in the here and now? So, here I am with that mask that smells of nothing and feels like cardboard, dreaming of a picnic in a field. Follow me with Rudd's glasses swinging back and forth, tick-tock like a pendulum. Characters come alive to me. There's fourteen-year-old Zera Preston. Already the eyes of the law are upon him. I read about the arms he holds. I picture him sullen, hugging his elbows to his body. He talks of other boys and of the gun in his hand, "a sort of musket from home." That "kind-of," "sort-of" gets me, this gummy, gluey language of teens. There are also two immigrants, Thomas Devyr, an Irishman who's fled from prison in Newcastle in the north of England, and William Brisbane, who's left Scotland. Devyr is a publisher and political organizer, and Brisbane a subtenant on a nearby farm—basically a tenant of a tenant farmer. He is the laborer who challenges the lawyer and sheriff at Moses Earle's auction. Devyr and Brisbane have both been in the United States for only five years. The two of them separately rally the Anti-Renters. There's Warren Scudder, too; Bluebeard, he's called, the Calico chief who heads to the showdown at Earle's farm in his father's cart. Bluebeard wields a silver-plated sword.

These men and boys are dispossessed. They carry guns, knives, axes, and something called a dirk, a long thrusting dagger from the Scottish Highlands. Some of the men have fled Scotland because of the Highland Clearances and the spread of feudalism. They are victims of capitalism and greed, as land—common land, everyone's land—is stolen and made into vast estates. In the Highlands, people have been burned out of their cottages because sheep are more valuable than people, more valuable than their smallholdings and common lands. During this time, in the United Kingdom if you don't have property, you cannot vote. Devyr has been arrested campaigning for this right to enfranchisement. There are also those men involved whose grandfathers fought in the revolution. Even with promised veterans' pensions, the men were so poor that they came west only to find themselves tenant farmers, not free at all. And, there is Augustus Kittle. His family all call him Gus.

Now in these two Januaries, it is the end of the month. We go to resistance meetings. Soup is shared in groups on Sunday afternoons. Anger tastes of butternut squash and split pea and bean chili. We protest ICE and other outrages. I write letters to the paper about my father and how a cross was burned on his lawn when he was little, how his grandparents came to the United States as economic migrants. Or just migrants. What is the difference between that day and this day, then and now?

David tells people he is a migrant, not that he is a citizen or immigrant, but a migrant.

In a census I find Augustus Kittle listed as a "laborer." Picture him, Gus, with his rust-red hair. I see him, long and lanky. What "laborer" means: no land and little future. That word is all I have of him.

The Anti-Renters talk of the revolution that will come at the ballot box or via a tar bucket. For a while all seems celebratory, and the Calico Indians wear their disguises to parties including on New Year's Eve, but really these men in the dresses are the enforcers. They will capture whoever bears the papers for a rent sale. Notices are torched, messengers tortured. It's the vigilante justice of the lynch mob. The enemy is rolled in pine tar and covered in feathers. One organizer says, "The gentlest means possible ought to be used, but failing that, use the gentlest means necessary."

At the end of January the governor outlaws disguises: The People of the State of New York, represented in Senate and Assembly, do enact as follows:

> Every person, who, having his face painted, discolored, covered, or concealed, or being otherwise disguised, in a manner calculated to prevent him from being identified . . . may be pursued and arrested.

The numbers of activities the law forbids go on and on. You can't meet, can't hide, can't gather in a tavern in a mask or disguise. Three or more people cannot gather, cannot carry an offensive weapon, a sword, or firearms. "Every law officer . . . or other citizen of the county"—that is, anyone cop or not—must arrest anyone in disguise "without process"; e.g., no due process. The third article gives sheriffs and other "peace officers," as they're called, the right to "command any male inhabitant . . . to assist him in seizing, arresting, confining and conveying . . . and committing to the common jail . . . every person with his face so painted, discolored covered or concealed." And, anyone who refuses to help will themselves be arrested and fined $250 (around $8,000 today).

No 8. This act shall take effect immediately. It is January 28, 1845.

———

At the women's march in Delhi, David holds up a sign that says "Sad" in Twitter's typeface. He stands with a German friend and the two discuss how bad things have to be here for them to return to their own countries. David says now as a citizen he has the right to happiness. The German adds, And guns. The German is not a citizen though he has been here half his life. David says, And did you know, when you become a citizen, they ask if you will take up arms for the United States?

———

Fight or die, the Calico Indians declare after the anti-masking law goes into effect. "They had either got to fight or die." Some burn the disguises and swear off their membership in the militia. Others become more militant. They spoil distress sales on February first, then again two weeks later, and again on March seventh.

Threats rise. It's neighbor vs. neighbor. Undersheriff Osman Steele baits the Anti-Renters and hectors crowds. He will come to a sale on horseback, flanked by followers. He'll appear too in the middle of the night and brutalize a man's wife to make her give up her husband. One historian calls him a "bully"; another writing early in the 1900s describes him as "bold, forward, officious." A couple of years before the war, he's arrested for battering a woman. As undersheriff he takes to the law just as he's taken to breaking it.

Now it is late winter, early spring 1845. He arrests a Roxbury farmer. In retaliation, the Indians kidnap Steele. He escapes his captors and flees to a tavern. The insurgents surround it. The sheriff sends a posse of some 200 men to free Steele. A couple days later Steele, the bullying bold undersheriff, goes on the rampage for revenge.

On the Ides of March he sets out again for Roxbury with the constable, his brother-in-law, Erastus Edgerton. They arrive in sleet and snow. The battles last for days. "OUR

COUNTRY HAS BEEN IN GREAT COMMOTION FOR ABOUT TEN DAYS PAST," the Delhi paper declares. The lawmen abduct Zera Preston. The alarm is raised; the teen cannot be taken; not to Delhi, not to prison, whether because he's so young or so integral to the cause, who knows?

The next day Edgerton and Steele fight it out with the Calico Indians on a bridge. Steele yanks a mask off one of them who turns out to be my town's constable.

With a dozen or so men under arrest, Steele carries them in a wagon the twenty-five miles to jail. En route he stops for libations and leaves his prisoners bound together, shivering outside and uncovered while he goes in for a drink to warm himself. In the bar he jokes about the cattle he's transporting.

—

It takes me time to learn all of this. At first the worlds of 1845 and today seem separate: protests and violence, Trump and these young men. But they grow together into one thing. What I originally know of this uprising is vague: a mural in the post office, the police dog, that parade, some highway signs decorated with the silhouette of someone in a dress with a horn. The legend: FREE SOIL. FREE PEOPLE.

How cute Ozzie, the dog named for Osman Steele, seems in news accounts reporting that he "joins" the force. But an uprising by poor tenant farmers now marked by a drug-sniffing dog in a drug crisis that hits the rural poor? Another line goes here with everything impossible to say with these gaps in time.

One day I go to the Delhi post office catty-corner from the courthouse. A WPA artist painted the mural there. It is dark and murky. There's a man on a white rearing steed and cartoonish protesters holding up a sign, "Down with Rent." Meanwhile a tiny boy out of scale with the rest floats like an angel in a black suit.

I take pictures of it, painted high to the ceiling and around moldings for a door engraved "Postmaster." A postal worker says to someone on the phone:

Clerk: Yes, the job is still open. Where are you calling from? (Pause. She waits for the answer.) Do you know where we are? (pause / response) It's a rural route, part-time. Snow. We get snow. Do you have your own car? You know about snow? You live where? New Jersey? Well, move up and then get in touch with us.

Something about money and work and desperation comes through the line without knowing the other side of the conversation. I guess that it's something about our long recession, still unending, still the results of the housing crisis, the loose lending and tightening credit, the rage, the frustrations.

I forget what I came to mail.

———

———

After days of searching in the county clerk's office, I finally find a tenant lease. It's between Augustus Kittle's aunt and uncle and Morgan Lewis. In 1837 the couple sign a document declaring they will pay Lewis rent on the first of February in bushels of "good clean sweet merchantable winter wheat." The language is dizzying. There are many adjectives and no commas in the deeds. I think of my students and their debt.

On the second page, I untangle florid demands for payment "yearly and every year" and "in each year thence succeeding" of ever more bushels of grain. The rent will rise until 1846, "and every year forever thereafter." Gus's uncle is to deliver "four hundred and eighty pounds weight equal to eight bushels" to the Hudson River. This on thirty-four acres of land so poor that growing any wheat is nearly impossible, given its two rocks for every dirt.

At the bottom is a place for Kittle's aunt to sign. Her mark is an *X*. A splotch spreads out where the ink has bled. I realize she can't read or write.

In the room with the people on the phone to banks and lawyers, I study the document's tight cursive. The lease talks of "exempting and recusing," a word that looks like *rescuing*. This recusing/rescue and exemption is, the document states, "always to the party aforesaid"—that is, to the landlord (and isn't it always for the one who has money?). What is kept aside for him are "all mill sites with two acres of ground adjoining the same the Sole and the Exclusive right of Erecting mills and mill dams Hereon: and also all mines, minerals and ores within the above [some illegible word which I think means "described"] premises."

The air is heavy; the voices stop. Or I stop hearing them. The weight that hits me: land, property, wealth. And why should I be shocked now? The United States is founded on property and wealth in people as property. These deeds reveal a world of early America where a second kind of enslavement exists. Here in the North, farmers are tied to the land in perpetuity, while people like Lewis and his colleagues, including Alexander Hamilton, find a language to make such peonage binding. The tenants are also, I soon learn, in a double bind. Their rents go to support slavery in the South and the Caribbean, where the flour the tenant farmers deliver is sent to feed people enslaved from Africa.

Glare from the lights overhead reflects off the table where I sit. I see the waterfall from that first day I walked up Bull Run. The landlord keeps these falls, and all falls, for himself and his heirs and assigns to own the right to manufacture, mill, and mine.

The lease goes on. It describes what will happen if Kittle and "his heirs and assigns" are ever behind in the rent: "It shall and may be lawful to [ ] reenter and distrain and the distress [spelled distrefs] and distrefses which shall be there and found and taken, to lead drive chose take or carry away impound and dispose of until the said rents and all arrears thereof (if any shall be) unto the party aforesaid of the first part his heirs and assigns be fully paid and satisfied."

This "distrain and distress"—those Ds and Ss and Rs roll together in a symphony of dolor. What they mean is that the landlord or his agent can come in anytime to make up the debt whenever they see fit. The distrain allows them to seize goods and then sell them at what is called a "distress sale." There's no need even to secure a court judgment.

In 1832 Morgan Lewis's original mansion in Staatsburgh, across the Hudson from me, is burned in an arson fire. Possibly by angry tenants.

—

Eighteen-thirty-seven or thirty-nine or forty-four. Twenty-ten, twenty-fourteen, twenty-sixteen. Recession and riots and here rural America revolts.

Augustus's aunt and uncle sign their lease in 1837, the same year as the Panic, the bank crisis that becomes everyone's crisis, with people going hungry, forced to cities for factory jobs with paltry and plummeting wages. There are no safety protections, no unions, no job security, no eight or ten or even twelve-hour workdays—even for kids. I read that in the UK, as soon as a child can crawl, they work. I am sure the same is true in New York and elsewhere. Meanwhile this crisis, the Panic, spreads from country to country. People flee to the United States, believing that this country will be better. And, in one sense it is. In the 1830s everyone gets the right to vote. That "everyone" is all white men. You no longer need land, property, to vote. Democracy spreads and with it cheap newspapers for every point of view.

—

Meanwhile I scroll the news, things called feeds. The internet is said to have democratized our lives.

I think of Austrian poet and writer Ingeborg Bachmann's aching novel *Malina*. Her first sentence: "'Today' is an impossible word for me . . . you can't escape it [. . .]. This today sends me flying into the utmost anxiety and the greatest haste. [. . .] In fact 'today' is a word that only suicides should be allowed to use." I read her "today" and my own day is porous and slipping. I add another note to my wall.

A friend asks what I'm so angry about. It is these things all together, wealth power and money, as well as the way poor white people's rage supports the party of the rich who are getting richer. Everything is linked, and I cannot separate these facts and turn them into narrative or trim them into story or plot.

In the deeds office in Delhi I'm in the room with a long wooden table. It gleams with a sheen from so many arms and elbows leaning on it for years. I think of Marx and his dancing tables in *Capital*. They begin as just wood, "an ordinary sensuous thing," he puts it, and then they become a commodity. They stand on their head, he writes, and dance—dance, dance, dance—as if of "their own free will." There are his "metaphysical subtleties and theological niceties." There is the low murmur of people talking to banks and lawyers about deeds and sales and mortgages. There's the mortgage crisis and my mortgage and how capital is used to help the wealthy over and over, how the idea of home ownership is to make something of nothing, to create a gap that grows and grows.

The woman from the thrift store is not here today.

On the land, the beavers halfheartedly try to fix the dam, mounding up a few sticks across the gap before giving up. But, the willows are gone, and so the socialist beavers have to go. They have to move. They leave, we learn, for our neighbors, who are also our friends, who have in their driveway the red, white, and blue hand-painted Trump sign that their kids make.

———

David is on the phone to his office. He's talking about something with an online platform. He hangs up and says he doesn't care about this platform or any other. He walks to the window and stares out at the stream, then walks downstairs and back. He hates the fleeting evanescence of selling things on a platform, selling soap or sunglasses, and the parties that the companies behind these products want to throw in order to have influencers attend so they post on this platform or another one. Outside he shovels the walk, though he's already shoveled it once and no new snow has fallen.

Chapter 15

IT'S MARCH AND I'M SITTING in another sap house with a few friends, one of them a county judge. I visited his courtroom when I was writing the crime novel. Someone passes what they call a mapletini. I am drinking a beer. The judge runs a hand through his sandy hair. His name comes from the Dutch for rose, and his was one of the first families to settle here centuries ago. He wears jeans and a sweatshirt emblazoned with the college his daughter attends. I think it's the first time I've ever seen him in casual clothes. Talk turns to the opioid crisis. Now, as family court judge, he gets only cases that relate to this crisis. In the store and on the street, I notice people skinny and jumpy. They are all edge and angle with faraway looks, and it looks familiar. There's a chaos I recognize, a jangling hinge in the air. The judge says something about Muriel's cousin or second cousin who has been living in her house. There's a mention of prescription drugs.

Someone puts a log on the stove; another puts the martini shaker out in the snow to stay cold. Froth rises on the boiling sap. At Muriel's, after the cousin or second cousin moves out, a dumpster sits outside in the snow and fills with furniture I recognize from her living room. I say something about how every other place I've lived in New York or London there have been addicts and now here. The judge says, So it's your fault; you're to blame, eh?

The judge laughs, others laugh, and I laugh. They aren't being cruel to me or the addicts, but what there is in all of these places is poverty. Something else jangles into this moment. It is gentrification, land and capitalism. That is part of what has followed me here—no matter what else.

———

That winter the forester dies, the one who complained of the politician's shoes. He's killed in a farming accident, helping a friend with a tractor. On a steep slope in the ice and snow, the machine rolls over on him. He dies instantly. To honor this man who has been logger of the year for the eastern United States, logging trucks parade down Main Street. Calling hours are in the central school's cafeteria. The line to enter is twenty, fifty people deep. The judge and his wife attend. Rudd and his partner attend. In line we talk of skiing. Inside, people mill with their own people, and all of them are interconnected in ways that are still opaque to us. We sit on the folding chairs and stand together on the outskirts, shy and apart, unsure what to say. The trucks park outside the school.

And, the bottle gentians are closed to outsiders.

I study the uprising, and in the spring before the trees leaf out, David and I use the HELPP and cut firewood together. He holds my hands and corrects my hinge.

Across my town and county, new residents arrive. They often come because they can't afford to buy in the city, so get a place upstate. They are designers, writers and editors, curators and gallerists—others who I have no idea what they do. There's a farmer who makes kimchi with her Korean-American family; another with a degree in Performance Studies from NYU who earns so little from farming she can't pay back her student loans. She campaigns for food justice and land trusts. Someone comes who paints the handles of axes. He's had, I hear, a breakup. The life crisis turns into catharsis and becomes a vocation or a business. The axes are marketed in the city as a connection to rural manliness and masculinity. They are meant to be displayed on walls.

There is talk about how it's getting harder and harder for people here to find places they can afford to live. Listings in the paper for rentals all but disappear, and still Muriel's old farmhouse goes empty after the relatives move out. In a community group on Facebook someone advertises an apartment for $1,500 a month, and the comments afterward say angry things about New York City. In the same group a month later someone else asks about the little biting flies of late May. Another person responds: Go back where you came from. And, now here are more and more people who are like me, or like I was in London, self-employed or freelance and working from home. I think of my dad and all the barbecue dinners and small-town events he went to in all these places he spent his life. Rudd says, The Catskills have always had new residents and tourists. That's our history.

On trucks SAVE THE LOCALS bumper stickers are replaced over time with ones pledging allegiance to the Second Amendment. Up Bull Run a sign goes up saying, NO TRESPASSING VIOLATORS WILL BE SHOT SURVIVORS WILL BE SHOT AGAIN. A posted sign and another for a home security company hang below. And, in the fields above the former beaver pond, the deer have started to eat the gentians. The tops have been chewed down, leaving bare stalks that refuse to bloom. The plants are so bitter, they're the only animals that can stomach the greens. Like a crazy woman, I yell at the deer. They glance at me with boredom and barely raise their heads.

—

I read these pages in a coffee shop in Delhi. A woman in a floaty dress with big sunglasses perched on her head and a cold brew in her hand laughs with another woman. Oh, where are you? the first woman asks. They both realize they have places here. Floaty dress: when we came we had this idea of a commune. The other says she did too. We are communists, the two laugh conspiratorially, as if there's something dangerous in the word. I look at my sandwich (expensive) and imported flavored water (fancy) and see my own judgments. I think about the letter Emerson wrote to Thomas Carlyle in the 1840s. "We are a little wild here with numberless projects of social reform," he says. Everyone "has a draft community in his waistcoat pocket."

Back then in the wake of the 1837 Panic one key element differs from today. The financial disaster spurs wide-ranging critiques of capitalism. Utopian alternatives are spun, and socialism spreads across the country. People believe in possibilities outside of capitalism. It is not a done deal yet, in the young America, and unlike the resignation I feel, where escaping capitalism seems impossible, people don't act like they have to accept it. There isn't a sense of inevitability about the free market, no belief that it must rule because it always has ruled. People think the world can be different—better—and that the American experiment is about embracing different and better. Collective values are more important than the self, and the word "individualism" comes into use. It's not meant as a bracing adjective for an American ethic of self-reliance but instead as a pejorative for those who seek their own benefit over others'.

People establish communes, communities, associations, families, and societies. The goal in each: live together collectively sharing property and labor. Shaker membership soars as people rush to join the celibate pacifists who renounce material goods for the greater common good. Not far from my parents' co-op are the Oneidas, not the Haudenosaunee nation, but the free-love practicing Christian perfectionists. Still another sect hews to the socialism of Jesus's early disciples and sets up just outside Buffalo. They have had to flee Germany and will go on to move to the prairies and become the Amanas.

Near Boston, Brook Farm is founded on the principle that all the participants will share in the proceeds and none will benefit more than the other. They believe all should receive healthcare, food, housing, and education. (Among the famous members: Nathanial Hawthorne.) A son of a wealthy New York landlord brings the ideas of French socialist Charles Fourier to the United States. Fourier has coined the word feminism and believes freedom is the kink that each of us has, and liberation means finding the partner for that kink. He also espouses living in collective phalanxes. They flourish; more than thirty phalanxes are formed across the country, including seven in Upstate New York.

By 1840, the Welsh industrialist-turned-socialist Robert Owen has already founded and failed in his utopian community New Harmony in Indiana, but his influence continues to grow. His ideas spark newspapers, nascent trade unions and time banks, where an hour of labor is worth an hour of labor and no capital is accrued or money exchanged. Other followers found communities dedicated to living Owen's values.

Chartists form in the UK. They're the first mass worker revolution. They battle to expand democracy—in Britain only the wealthy can vote. Their tactics call for fighting in cells with members known only to each other, and their plans include land trusts—land co-operatives essentially. They will undermine feudalism by establishing a new commons so all have property—and the vote. Just outside Manchester, the first co-operative is also established. Twenty-eight flannel weavers, two of them women, start the Rochdale Equitable Pioneers. It's an experiment in joint ownership. The name alone signals their values. "Equitable" means cutting out the middlemen, the capitalists, making money off the poor, and these people are poor. I grow up hearing stories of them. My parents' co-op is still run on the Rochdale Principles.

The weavers are in debt to grocers who dilute their flour with sawdust. The grain is full of weevils, and the grocers have one price for cash, another for credit. Credit always higher. These debts will always increase. The weavers are too poor to pay cash. The word "Pioneer" in their name comes from the UK's first trade union newspaper. To be an equitable pioneer is to put a stake in the ground for change. They open a grocery store, one where they are all joint owners and they buy directly from their suppliers, paying fair prices without a capitalist's markup.

They get a nod in Marx's *Capital* when it comes out a few years later. The members are also Owenites, Chartists, and Temperance workers. Many have been arrested already for trying to form unions. They call themselves "co-operators," a word I love, and "Co-operative" is always capitalized. It is a direct democracy, one person, one vote, my father tells me often, even for the women.

These groups all have one thing in common. They are supported by Horace Greeley. He runs a weekly column on Fourierites in the *New-York Tribune*; Karl Marx becomes his European columnist, and in the United States Greeley publishes *Self Help by the People*—the first book on the Rochdale Pioneers. I read in its pages about how they "rearrange the powers of production and distribution" and see my parents young and exuberant in their new life at the co-op. How happy they were, how free, and then there's all that my mom sacrifices for their dream. My dad too, forfeiting a connection to his children, and she lives in her anger and frustration.

What is it like to exist in simmering rage, her rage, and how it became mine too with the fights with my dad? Or what is it like to live here in rage? The new people often rent out their places on Airbnb or VRBO to make back their mortgage costs or so they can also afford their rent in the city. That leaves less housing available for those who have been here, who work here. And, there is the Chomsky quote on the wall, the paper curling in the humidity of summer. Chomsky channeling that voice of despair. "I'm getting shafted." We all are.

———

It is August, David's birthday. I have to wait for a shipment from my parents' home that day. My sister has been settling the estate. I have promised David we can go for a hike and a swim across a lake, just a day together, not his work, not the stress or the flash of posts flitting and disappearing, tied to a multinational corporation's metrics. Instead we must wait for things, including my mother's rocker, to arrive. The trucking company gives us a window from ten until two. They arrive at three, so there will be no swim and no hike.

Late that afternoon without planning where we are going, we head up Bull Run, which set me on this path twelve years earlier. We pass the hairpin turn. Light cracks through the trees. It doesn't feel like hope or a John Denver song today. The treetops bow ominously, shaking their fringed boughs. I ask David if he wants to climb down to the waterfall.

"Nah."

He kicks at a rock and we are silent at each other. Along the road wild parsnip grows. It is poisonous. It burns the skin. There are asters, goldenrod, and Queen Anne's lace. I want to ask what he is thinking; I want to tell him about the deeds and the land. I want him to say he forgives me. Then I want to ask what he looks forward to in this next year—an insistent question I pose at every birthday. I don't.

I pause and watch him, think of the bushels of wheat and of money. Lewis and Livingston owned this stream, and the water was money. It was a mill. The income must have been negligible. Still it allows them to earn off Clum and Kittle and their neighbors' grain, even before the rent.

I want to tell David all of that and to talk of skinny-dipping alone in brooks like this when I was little. The moment passes and we walk by Muriel's farm. The SURGE MILKER sign is gone. Hank is too sick to come up. Their kids don't either. One daughter comes one weekend this summer. A rhododendron towers over the porch and crowds the tiny house.

We walk up the lane and past Muriel's blackberries. The stones are silent, the goldenrod is silent, and David is silent.

The poet Ian Parks writes of goldenrod:

The wind blows through the goldenrod
as death flows through a crowd.
Nothing is accomplished,
and the world is changed by it.

———

That night we stay in the tent. Sometime after dark when David is asleep, I hear the siren, and coyotes howl in response. At 4 a.m., owls hoot asking each other *who-who-who looks for you*. One responds with a cawing sound as if they are chattering to each other: *Beware, beware, beware*.

Chapter 16

THE MAN COMES TO ME in the dark from more than a century away. His gaze burns through time. He sits with a friend. The friend on the left is blurred; the friend can't sit still long enough for the exposure, but it is he, the one on the right, I see. His penetrating stare holds the camera and me. He is blazingly handsome with tousled hair, and he doesn't flinch—or I don't, and it is something about his composure that stops me.

The men are held in their moment. They wear the clothes of their age—the high collars and long jackets, and it is despite those things that he arrives. It is the slouch, the easy intimacy between them as their shoulders touch, the hands in the lap, and the stare. It is also, of all things, their plaid trousers. The longer I look, the more I'm convinced they're velvet. I study his knee and can pick out the texture, can almost feel the fabric through the screen. This man in his early twenties feels like he belongs to today, with the sex and swagger of youth.

He is Jay Gould. He will go on to become a railway baron, a robber baron, famous in his time for watering stocks, though he is not one of these magnates we hear of, not Cornelius Vanderbilt or J. P. Morgan or a Rockefeller. In the decade after the Civil War, Gould will spur a run on gold that sparks a recession and then deploy Pinkertons to crush strikes.

Right now at this moment, in this picture with its irrepressible power, those events are fifteen or more years into the future. He lives in Roxbury where the first battles of the Anti-Rent War take place, and poses with his friend and neighbor Hamilton Burhans. Gould is writing the first account of the uprising. It's going to be part of his *History of Delaware County* that will be published in 1856, just a decade after the fighting ends. The book's long and florid subtitle goes on for lines, promising: *"A HISTORY OF THE LATE ANTI-RENT DIFFICULTIES IN DELAWARE, With Other Historical and Miscellaneous Matter NEVER BEFORE PUBLISHED."*

In those pages he describes Mr. John B Gould, his father, who is "up-rent," who supports the landlords. His dad owns a tavern. One summer day in 1844, the Calico Indians come to teach him a lesson:

> The savage horde sprung from their hiding places, and with demonlike yells rushed up and surrounded Mr. Gould, who was standing with his little son in the open air in front of the house.

> We were that son: and [. . .] they surrounded that parent with fifteen guns poised within a few feet of his head, while the chief stood over him with fierce gesticulations, and sword drawn. 0, the agony of

my youthful mind, as I expected every moment to behold him prostrated a lifeless corpse upon the ground. His doting care and parental love had endeared him to his family. But he stood his ground firmly; he never yielded an inch.

We were that son. I see Jay Gould as a little boy, nine years old and terrified. His father lives. He's a member of the "law-and-order party" just like conservatives now, proclaiming their allegiance to the police. Of course, the young Gould despises the Calico Indians. He calls them an "incubus" with "treasonable designs."

Then he goes on, "Still another class, followers of Fourier and Owen, world-conventionists, who gave a ready support to every scheme, however wide from nature, or wanting in common sense . . . gave them their sympathy and assistance."

I'm reading on my laptop. The cursor blinks; words flash from his time to my time. Gould is saying the Calico Indians are radicals, essentially that they, like my parents and their co-ops, are followers of Owen and Fourier, the people responsible for the most radical ideas in the United States at the time.

David is on the phone with his office—it's about something for skin or hair, for men or women or both, something with battle ropes and soap or deodorant, something that will stop you sweating for forty-eight or seventy-two hours, a period so long it should cause cancer or kill you, but instead for some multinational corporation this will be money, sales, that will require David to manage a shoot in a gym with perspiration on bodies and faces glistening and gleaming but not the underarms, not sweat, not there, not smell. This ad or not-ad, this post, will flicker and disappear on a platform, on the democratizing internet. Outside the siren on the fire hall blares. It is noon.

I tell David about the Anti-Renters being socialists. He is used to my obsession by now. "They align with Charles Fourier," I say, my voice rising, "and Robert Owen." I tell him who Fourier and Owen are. Owen, I am saying, this is *the* Robert Owen, with a stress on the "this" and "the." I say that he is Welsh, as if David, half Welsh himself, should claim the connection.

My tenses slip. It is lunchtime. He makes sandwiches. I picture Owen with his lamb-chop sideburns and Fourier, coining feminism and supporting orgies, alongside my neighbors in swirling dresses, prim Shakers in their bonnets, and the free-love Oneidas. There are the co-operators too—and that woman in the floaty dress. Then there is Gould in his plaid velvet trousers with his friend.

I lose time to the *New York Times*, scrolling through headlines about Gould from the nineteenth century. He's so despised he's assaulted on the street by strangers not once but twice.

David is across the office and he faces a screen, and I stare into 1877, a year that is the start of another depression, the Long Depression, that will last into the 1890s.

MR. JAY GOULD ASSAULTED.
HE IS CHASTISED ON THE STREET.
A HUGE AND INDIGNANT BROKER

*MEETS THE LITTLE MAN IN THE
STREET, AND A QUARREL ENSUES—
THE LATTER MORE FRIGHTENED
THAN HURT—WHAT LED TO THE
DIFFICULTY—GOULD CHARGED
WITH DECEIVING HIS FRIENDS—
STATEMENTS BY THE PARTIES
INTERESTED.*

Or, at the Haymarket trial in Chicago in 1886, where the anarchists on the stand make a joke about Gould. The judge tells the spectators, "When you are so tickled you cannot restrain yourselves you can go out doors." The rest of the afternoon, the *Times* reports, is taken up with reading headlines and articles from various "Socialist organs. The theme of the articles read was revolution."

Revolution: 1845, 1886, 1965, 2011, 2016, 2017.

Another article, another day of the same anarchists' trial, someone testifies that the crowd calls out to hang Gould, another to throw him in the lake. (This lake is Lake Michigan; the taunts are metaphor or hyperbole. Gould is not present.) It is July 27, 1886. One testifies, "If Jay Gould was put out to-day another Jay Gould or 100 Jay Goulds would rise up. It is the system that ought to be destroyed."

The system needs to be destroyed, I agree, and our afternoons should be taken up with discussions of socialism. I feel as if nothing has changed—or that all the changes in the intervening years have disappeared. Now the three richest Americans have more money than half the country put together.

The *Times* writes that a woman "in a dress of white lawn comes to the courthouse early." She runs to the prisoners when they're brought in, "tendering each one of them a bunch of flowers." I want to tender flowers. I want tender flowers, I want to celebrate the woman in the white lawn dress there in a Chicago court.

Now I swim in the pool Gould's fortune paid for. In his lifetime he doesn't give much to charity. There are no Gould libraries like Andrew Carnegie founds, no museums bearing his name. In his hometown, Roxbury, he endows a single church, but his family establishes a rec center here in 2014. I call it the "robber baron swimming pool" and am grateful for a place to swim laps.

Before she dies, my mom comes to visit, and I tell her about the Gould pool that's just being built. We drive through Roxbury. I point out the church, and she hums a song, "Jay Gould's Daughter," about his child's greed. In fact, he has two daughters, one of lavish means who marries into European ancestry—the one, I'm sure, of the song—and the other who is pious and anti-communist and spends her summer here. She gives to many charities and also builds a golf course for her private use. We pass its entrance, and in her quavering voice my mom sings:

> Jay Gould's daughter said before she died.
> Papa fix the blinds so the bums can't ride.

She raised me on folk songs about protest and the poor. I read somewhere a rumor that Cornelius Vanderbilt built Grand Central to one-up Gould as a grand fuck-you.

The Gould great-grandson who finances the pool also collects houses here, entire farms. He buys them up in a remote valley to preserve them. All of the land is posted, even the waterfalls. If you stop to look at them, if you get off your bike, say, to see how the water has, over millennia, carved rocks into a dramatic channel, a security person will materialize and tell you to move on.

At the pool I think of Gould, my mom, the anarchists, and how all this money has traveled through time. Swimming can feel like flying, with the glide of fingertips stroking the water.

Sometimes I see a stooped man on the pool deck in the loose-waisted trousers of the elderly. He has a walker and stands with a woman my sisters' age. I realize this is the Gould who built the pool, and he's here with his daughter, Jay Gould's great-, great-, great-, his 3x great-granddaughter. The man smiles and takes in the scene, thrilled to see us all swimming. The pool is no Grand Central. It has a metal shed roof and one dying palm a lifeguard drags in. I love the sight of father and daughter together. I picture my mom in the car. She was ecstatic in her glory, this eighty-something-year-old woman singing aloud as I drove. The Queen Anne's lace bobbed in our wake.

I play Pete Seeger's version of the song for David on YouTube.

If ride they must, they got to ride the rod
Let 'em put their trust in the hands of God

In the pool I do a flip turn and steady myself by staring at the lane markers. Blue chlorine, black tiles, and the hands of God. In the water David looks like a seal. I hope swimming makes him less anxious about the work he's finding harder and harder to do.

I ask the Gould great-great at a fundraiser for the gym if it's true about Grand Central, and she says, yes, well, the men certainly were rivals.

———

In Gould's book there's this phrase, "world convention-ists," I've never heard before. It sounds to me like "internationalism," which later in the nineteenth century becomes the code word for the global left—anarchists and socialists and those seeking to overturn the injustices of the Gilded Age. The anarchists on trial for the Haymarket Riots in 1886 are "internationalists" in the *Times*. But, Gould writes this forty years before, in 1845, and these are my neighbors. I want to understand just what the phrase means.

In 1847:

THE LITERARY WORLD.
A Gazette for
AUTHORS, READERS, AND
PUBLISHERS

lists, "The English 'liberal,' 'peace man,' 'philanthropist,' 'world's conventionist' 'cosmoplite' & c.," Those scare quotes and the "and cetera" make it pretty clear the phrase is a way to diss the Left—the ridiculous dreamers and schemers of change. They are my kin, my community, affinity . . . They are Chartists, co-operators, and Anti-Renters, and they are organizing four years before the Revolutions of 1848 and the *Communist Manifesto*, here in this hill country with its two rocks for every dirt.

—

On the street, in the CVS, in the Foodtown—the same grocery chain I shop at in Brooklyn when I'm in the city to teach—I stand in the produce aisle. A woman in silver Birkenstocks rushes past. Her child drifts away and calls out. A man I recognize from a TV show on HBO studies the beers on offer. There are two dozen different IPAs from craft breweries. The store's piped in music plays the Clash. It's "The Guns of Brixton." I almost laugh. Guns and revolution in my old neighborhood in London. And here too. I have a basket of avocados and a six-pack of beer. And, I have a secret—I have Rudd and that mask.

—

The Anti-Renters don't work in isolation. They're not just farmers in hill country going broke. Anti-Rent newspapers are published in Delhi, Albany, *and* Brooklyn.

The Delhi organ is the *Voice of the People*. In very small type the strapline declares: NOT FOR ME, BUT FOR MY COUNTRYMEN. I read that subhead with its implication of doing for others, of the collective and communal over the individual, and my heart lifts.

The Albany paper is called the *Albany Freeholder* and champions land reform as the path to freedom. It's edited by Thomas Ainge Devyr, an Irish Chartist who escapes English prison. He's been indicted and arrested for sedition, and he walks to freedom, like Sojourner Truth. In Newcastle he and his wife board a boat bound for the United States. The ship is called the *Independence*, which comes to seem an irony. In America he finds little freedom for anyone. He lives in Williamsburg and begins touring tenant farms upstate. There he discovers the same tyranny he'd fought at home.

He knows that the Anti-Renters need to build a broader coalition. In the *Freeholder* he argues to: "Unite the farmer, the laborer, the mechanic in one solid phalanx. Their interests are the same." He travels from town to town giving speeches, and people across three counties come to hear him. He talks about the wealthy "becoming masters of the country," and how that wealth creates "a certain order of cause and effect." It becomes "'law and order,'" he says. "Rapacity and wrong will assume all the due forms of 'law and order.'" He talks of "oppression" as well, and how we, his listeners and our descendants, bound to these leases, are "enslaved."

In Brooklyn, he gets others involved and cofounds a group called the NRA, the National Reform Association. Another founder is the editor of an Owenite newspaper; his brother is a Shaker elder. Radical values run in the family. The NRA's slogan is VOTE YOURSELF A FARM! and the group wants to redistribute land as a way to redistribute wealth. The Reformers stand too for women's suffrage and abolishing slavery, and they demand a ten-hour workday. They also fight against nativism, against prejudice, and the rising anti-immigrant riots. In his 1847 *Principles of Communism*, Engels will claim allegiance with them.

I get this glinting feeling, a kaleidoscoping sense of possibility. What the Anti-Renters are trying to do is as radical as the dozens of utopian communes burgeoning across New York State in the 1840s. They are also certainly more violent.

This NRA, not of guns but reform, also supports bloodshed—if it comes to that. And, on the other side of the "if" are tar buckets, guns, and swords. "Don't you see the ball a-rolling?" one upstate NRA member says; he is a doctor in my town. One of the organizers calls for change "by political action, or, in failure of that, by revolution." The group holds their first convention in May 1845 in a hall on lower Bowery at Division Street. A who's who of radical America attends. There is Horace Greeley and the abolitionist Gerrit Smith, as well as the person who imported Fourier's ideas to the United States. The speakers include Robert Owen and the doctor from my town.

"No man made the land," Owen says in his speech, "no man could give title to it." The doctor addresses the group at "the forepart of May the 5th." I have no idea what he says to the crowd, but five days later the Anti-Renters hold an Equal Rights Convention in my county and the doctor advocates destroying the landlords.

Neighbors write letters to Devyr at the *Freeholder*. One praises a pamphlet Devyr penned before escaping Britain and mentions as an aside that he'd heard "you now lived at Williamsburgh." NRA organizers also live in Bushwick. Now again there are people coming up here from Williamsburg and Bushwick. Online, the leaflet's pages appear stained with age. It proclaims equality will come from destroying the aristocracy. My neighbors side with Chartists. I do too. And so do those first co-operators, the Rochdale Pioneers. My neighbors pen odes and poems. One anonymous poet from my town contributes regularly to the *Freeholder*. He writes the "Afflicted Tenant's Appeal" on July first and the next day "The Farming Men."

> Down rent your glorious watchword be,
> Freedom is in the sound;
> Proclaim with trumpet loud and free
> The welcome tidings round.

I read this, and one gap closes, the division I have felt in my two lives—upstate and down, urban and rural. Once, at least, they were united.

—

It is May. David has to return to London in a month for his shoot. It's already making him anxious. He sits on the stairs in our kitchen and stares at his knees. There's a bottle of beer on the floor. It is 4 p.m., 5 p.m. The condensation drips down the glass. There is news on the radio, some abounding atrocity in a current administration, and of the ephemeral realm of social media, of commodifying the evanescent. These things are always of this moment, which is always a past moment, which always slips, which always holds death because the moment is always over, always gone, because we are always rushing forward toward progress. And, David is swimming to keep up with the tides.

I say to him "sweetie." I try to make my voice gentle so it curves around him. I wonder how long he has been sitting there staring at his knees.

I've always had problems with tenses. They've always confused me. The past is all present, everything connected with no plot. And, so here we are with David on the stairs.

His feet are bare on ugly carpet that we have never removed. We have been too lazy maybe, or it is just not ugly
enough. His toes are long, elegant; and now we are soon to
move to the recreation of my parents' home up the road.

Weight balloons around us like a thought bubble full
of what is unsaid and unwritten. I try to cajole him into
telling me what is wrong.

At the pool I look over at David, so calm and long in the
water. He never creates a wave, and I am sure that swimming will do him good. *Freedom is in the sound; The wel-
come tidings round.*

Rudd tells me about his relative Harvey, the one in the
Anti-Rent War. He doesn't know much about him,
just that he was a scoundrel later. No good, he came to
no good, Rudd says with his chewed-down words. His
brother Burr emails a picture of him in his Civil War
uniform. On my screen Harvey's eyes glance up at something overhead, just out of the frame. He has a ring on
his left pinky finger; the buttons of his wool jacket are
undone at the waist so he can sit. I wonder what he sees,
what catches his attention during the long minutes he has
to stay still for the camera. Nineteen seconds, twenty-
five seconds, fifty-three . . . He focuses above him, on a
beam, maybe. One minute and three seconds, one minute
fifty-two seconds, fifty-seven, two minutes. He alights on

something in the middle distance, and something in his gaze looks divine, meditative.

He was dissolute, a drinker, Burr writes, and is arrested for forgery in the 1870s, I find. Which is to say, I find nothing, not really, just this three-quarter view turned to the camera. I imagine he is depressed, he has been through an unspeakable war. One arm is propped on a leg, and the background is blurred behind him. I think I see a tree, clouds painted on the studio wall. He's thirty-six, with wavy hair, and looks much younger. There's dirt on his shirt and his jacket. He is unyielding, and yet this man comes through the century to sit with me.

Upstairs in the sunroom a solitary red bloom appears on the plant with the dangerous sap. I think of what those men in the 1840s would look like on TV if we could see them now—the absurdity of it, fishing but not fishing, the dresses, the drag, and how in the moment I write drag is now politicized. Outside a pair of motorcycles screech down my street. The engines' high-pitched thrums sound like wasps. I picture the men in their helmets and T-shirts lumbering about in these dresses. I picture them spinning about in comic rage—the skirts billowing and flaring around them, the calico and its amoebas swimming across the fabric.

—

David texts photos from his shoot. There are shots of gyms, people with glorious, gleaming muscles. We talk. I scroll through his posts. We speak on a messaging service owned by a young billionaire. Our conversations drift and don't connect while he is away.

Chapter 17

THE LETTER IS ADDRESSED FROM CAMP, OF, THE, LEATHERHEADS, ROCKY, MOUNTAINS, 8, MOON and looks like a ransom note. The Calico Indians send it calling themselves "leatherheads." The archivist lays the paper carefully before me. The letters are in all caps with a comma after each word to disguise the handwriting. From this distance there's something comic and ridiculous in the careful penmanship that maybe isn't funny all. Maybe it is just terrifying, like speech threatening to kidnap a governor or hang a vice president, or a swastika online inside a Star of David, emblazoned under Twitter's blue bird proclaiming free speech.

I wear white cotton gloves to protect the sheet. It's lined and fragile, stained with splotches of ink and age and folded into thirds. I'm guessing it is August in that eighth moon. The term "leatherheads" makes me think of fans of gay leather bars, which I prefer to the Anti-Renters calling themselves "Indians." The note is sent to G. H. Edgerton, Erastus Edgerton's father. Erastus is Osman Steele's sidekick. G. H. runs a hotel here in Delhi, and the historical society also has receipts for things he buys in New York City, carpet and supplies for the hotel, stocks of alcohol. In the local paper are notices for sheriff's auctions on his premises.

The letter reads: "YOU ARE REQUESTED NOT TO MEDDLE PLOT NOR PLAN WITH THE LANDLORDS OR THEIR AGENTS LIKEWISE TO SETTLE UP ALL DIFFICULTIES WITH

ALL TENANTS OWNING OR OCUPING [I think this means oc-
cupying] SUCH [there is another "all" added in superscript,
so "all such"] LANDS BE ASSURED THAT THIS WARNING IS
NOT FOR NOTHING IF T A R AN F E A T H R [an E is added
in subscript for feather] WANT [won't] MAKE YOU STOP YOUR
ROBBERIES A TOUCH OF THE HAK [which I'm sure is an ax,
most of the Calico warriors carry them] OR A DOSE OF PISTLS
PILS WILL CURE YOU OF YOUR DISORDER [there is a particular flourish in the R of disorder like this: ℛ but even more
rococo. More curls on the tail]. T A K E   C A R E [the writer
warns] T H E   P U B L I C K   F E E L I N G   I S   A G A I N S T
Y O U. It is signed TAR and FETHERD.

———

There are ten thousand Calico Indians spread across
Upstate New York. But I want to draw a line around my
neighbors. Round characters come with traits I can't control and also can't overlook. I need though some understanding of what their appropriation means. Obviously
that isn't their word. They just use "Indians," and it's a long,
long line of people donning redface in the United States;
still, I have to find an answer. I need them to be heroic. I
am desperate to find shared values in this place. Because of
the way the past resounds into the present for me, I can't
abide their flaws and the racism inherent in their behavior.
I want them to exist not just in their time but mine.

I ask Rudd about the disguises and the name. He says
he doesn't know the reason for the name, but the calico
is because it was cheap. His brother Burr tells me about
a relative in the Boston Tea Party. Those men dressed as
Mohawks, the Kanien'kehà:ka whose lands also border
our town.

Here, where the sachem Cacawalemin lived, my neighbors fight to get the land they live on, land they feel is theirs, land that is stolen from the Lenape people, the Esopus tribe of the Munsee—and further to the north and west in this same patent, the Hardenbergh Patent, from the Mohawks and Oneidas of the Haudenosaunee. All of whom share property communally, whose leaders are chosen by women, where people have consensus democracy instead of majority rule. The National Reformers, like most of the other socialist utopians of the 1840s, dream of creating just this. The NRA wants collective agrarian towns, with no central politics or decision-making, yet that already exists in New York. These values are central to Indigenous peoples here. Meanwhile, Indian Removal policies try and fail to push the Haudenosaunee out of Upstate New York entirely but still manage to strip them of their most valuable land. Just at this moment in Buffalo, NY, the Seneca are coerced into signing a treaty by which they lose all claims to the city, their homeland, as it becomes the world's largest grain port and a center for American capitalism. They are also forced to adopt something akin to the US Constitution and voting, which is arguably less democratic than the system the Seneca already have.

I think back to those paintings at the Met, all those voices, those car ads, the West open and available, a frontier, pioneers, etc., etc. By erasing the people who are here or making them so small, they become adjuncts to a landscape, part of nature, part of a wilderness—which is to say invisible. All of these utopian schemes and dreams seem possible in the nascent United States because these communitarians and associationists don't see who lives here already.

—

I read an account of the Hardenbergh Patent being surveyed in the 1740s and how the Lenape throw the stones used as survey markers into the river, the one that flows through the center of my town, the East Branch of the Delaware River. The surveyor has laid them at sites of Lenape settlements, he writes. One "at an oyld Inden setelment where there is an orchard. The place is cal'd Pawpachton." Another at a settlement "Pawcawtocking." Then he and his comrades head west and steal a canoe. The canoe tips over, I read. Justice, I think. Then, their chains to measure distances in their metes and bounds get rusty. Yet on the men go and are confronted by enraged Indigenous residents. These surveyors promise that they're not surveying, because look at the rust? How could we? So, they lie and deceive to get the land.

Here Pakatakan, the mountain, is meant to mark where Cacawalemin had lived. Its name means either "he makes it clear" or "marriage of the waters." The mountain is neither clear nor a place where streams meet, not exactly, though three different creeks all drain into the river in Margaretville, making it a floodplain. That water all flows into the Pepacton, New York City's reservoir. Its name means "the sweet flag place," where calamus flowers grow. I think of Walt Whitman's "Calamus," the sweet flag like an erect cock in his poem.

In the early settlers' testimony Cacawalemin is often identified only as Hendrick Hekan, his adopted name, and those apple trees, I realize, are about property disputes. White officials are trying to figure out the borders of the Hardenbergh Patent. Apple trees were often planted at

surveyor's boundary lines. These white men all testify after
he was dead in order to make the ownership a fait accompli.

It is late May, and the heat has come so fast and early even
the grass wilts. I am walking to Steve Miller's over New
York City land. I once got lost here in winter. I was alone.
David was away and I was out snowshoeing. Stubbornly, I
wouldn't follow my tracks back the way I came, sure I knew
where I was heading even though the sun, which should
have been to my right, was behind me. I followed a deer
trail, thinking it was a path even though I knew better. I
came out miles away by a white farmhouse and was too
embarrassed to ask for help. I vaguely knew the couple who
lived there. I rushed down their lane and past Steve and
Jane's carrying my snowshoes on the plowed streets. Later,
I told them, and Jane said, Oh dearest, in her voice that
could hold me like a hug. Always come here first. She told
where they hide the keys.

Now I follow a logging road through the woods. Near
a spring where the ground is still damp, an eft, that animal
with its sense of time and home held in its body, rushes to
hide. In the distance, aspens, with their single collective
body from which all sprout as a clone, are leafing out. The
tops look like a cotton ball suspended in the trees—or a
cloud caught in the branches. I think about Devyr being
arrested for sedition and walking to freedom. I walk over
this mountain, and I think too how he comes to the United
States and is heartbroken by the lack of freedom he sees,
yet he fights for a change in a place where he is new.

Upstate, he visits the sort of people, poor white farmers, who could be quoted by Chomsky about all of us getting

screwed, and Devyr talks of riot or revolution, and I emerge from the woods. The leaves from last fall haven't decomposed. They rustle with each step. I duck past a neighbor's no-trespassing sign. Devyr sees how property is power, "cause and effect," he puts it. He proclaims too that non-violence is "bad policy." These moments stream together. They are vertiginous and dizzying, as if time and memory and history are held in the ground, right here on Kettle hill named for Kittle and his family. Now I sit with Steve outside on his porch in this replica of his parents' home.

He wears a plaid shirt and brushes at the sweat on his brow with a handkerchief. We drink iced tea. The deer have been birthing fawns in his potato fields. One this morning, Jane says, lay down right outside the kitchen before pulling herself up the hill. Steve tells me the does like fields; coyotes can't run in tall grass. I tell him I'm writing about the Anti-Rent War, and he nods vigorously. In his gravelly voice, he runs through a breathless blur of connections and cousins and uncles and greats and grands, all too fast for me to write down. He goes all the way back to the woman who drags Earle inside, who takes his wallet, who is staunchly Anti-Rent and won't let him pay his rent despite the mounting violence. Maybe without her nobody would have been shot. Steve says she and Earle are distant relations of his. All of these connections hurtle at me.

—

The alarm sounds on the fire hall, and it is 12:17 p.m. on my phone as I sit on the porch, and it is 1845. Then later it is 4:38 in the morning and the air raid circles again. The blinking alarm clock casts a pale green glow where we sleep in the turret with its bulge in the queenly house. Sirens race up the hill. I stare at the ceiling. I listen to hear if David is awake and feel guilty that I have not answered the call in an emergency. I think of a moment in the grocery store years earlier. The checkout clerk, a teenager resplendent with freckles and red hair, said, You live in the place on the corner, right? Yeah, yes, I nod. David is next to me, bagging our groceries. She says, I love your house. I grin. I am thrilled at this moment of connection or that she likes it, or maybe likes me. Some other beat of joy goes here, of this moment shared, before she says her family went to look at it when it was for sale but they couldn't afford it. I am still smiling, only the smile is something else, something frozen. I look down at the conveyor, at our groceries. A gallon of milk trundles past. I want to apologize. I focus on the carton's logo of a cow leaping over the earth. Everything that feels impossible to say is in this moment too. She isn't angry. It is a fact. This fact and the sound of her voice, which is warm and generous, break my heart.

Steve brings me a picture of himself as a baby. He's fat and happy in his mother's arms. He tells me stories of his father working three jobs, and Steve too as a boy, how he raised potatoes in the field below, and I think of Shirley who has said, We were all poor but didn't know it.

Later I look at pictures of my great-grandparents on my mother's side, dirt farmers—the image is like a WPA photograph, bleak and black and white. The couple in the shot are skinny and hard-bitten. She has her arms wrapped tight around her, he his hands splayed on his knees. He has a long, drooping mustache. She looks at the camera. The porch sags. At their feet are rocks. There's nothing pretty or quaint, no flower beds put in to dress up the house. The arms-wrapped woman in her apron probably has no time for flowers. Once I asked my mom if they'd had a car or tractor, and she laughed. Oh honey, they were too poor for that. They didn't have a car. They had a cart.

These reformers, the NRA, invite everyone into their movement: "Christians, Mormons, Infidels [. . .] anti-Slavery men, Associationists, Communitists, Temperance men, Peace men, Free Trade men, Free Land men." Not to mention: "Friends of Universal Freedom, Universal Education, Universal Homes, Universal Plenty, Universal Labor, Universal Happiness." This very list of all the people—indeed all these men (but I'm assuming women too) and faiths—everyone, "communitists" even, are included. That very word "communitist," which is an anachronism and was maybe never even an actual word except for in that moment on this list, is funny, at least to me. Then, that all of these "universals" and "friends" end on happiness, as if the ultimate good. But this is a different right to happiness than the Declaration of Independence promises. It's not tied to property but to sharing. I wonder what if rural rage could be linked to something like this today, instead of channeling anger into narrow visions of who belongs? What if the goal were bigger and broader? What if it were to include joy?

In these dreams from the nineteenth century is something like socialist anarchism. If we all have an equal share, we need no government because government—our government and European ones—supports wealth and hierarchies. Just look at the Constitution framed by men with land, ensuring those men can keep other humans as property. Reading about the NRA, I get this rousing brass-band oompah sense of possibility, of a different world, and in this world they are conjuring, they say that liberty is a right not to unlimited wealth but to something that is for all. "Steamboats and Rail Roads would be taken possession of [by] the people, and the whole population might have access to the beauties of Nature, which are now as a sealed book, except to a favored few."

The historian Mark Lause writes that the National Reformers promise a "libertarian socialist future." It sounds like the future my parents campaigned for. I find a speech of my dad's where he talks of the public over the private good, saying that natural resources belong to us all. There's another where he decries the mine, mine, mine, of individualism, and on the eve of his moving to Washington he writes a friend, another co-operator, that he is "going with great reluctance." He is just waiting for the time to go back to managing a co-operative, he writes, because "Being a Co-op manager is one of the most challenging and most satisfying positions a young man can have."

—

Steve says he wonders if people in the Anti-Rent War here got hijacked to someone else's political movement. In my need for these people to be heroic, this is maybe history or story, or just the narrative I need to tell with that gun waiting to go off.

Devyr the Brooklynite will be the one to call for "The gentlest means possible . . . but failing that use the gentlest means that might be necessary." The NRA will call for change at the ballot box or with a bullet box, and their critique of US democracy that preserving wealth means preserving poverty seems trenchant now. They say too, "If force is used to execute such laws, then force is justifiable in resisting their execution."

I read Devyr's obituary now in the *Brooklyn Eagle*.

Chapter 18

After a spring of snow, we have a summer of droughts. There are warnings of forest fires. Crops fail. We go to the shed/shack, and in the crumbling foundation, David finds a patent medicine bottle with moss and a fern growing in it like a terrarium, as if this could contain the world.

I want to think of David and me and my parents in this world. I am so near to where they'd lived and been happy. Early in the morning and late at night I pack boxes for the move. I try to do it myself because David has to leave again for work. While he is away, I help out at the annual carnival that the volunteer fire department sponsors. At the fair kids scream on rides and lights pierce the sky. A shooting gallery gives away fluffy plush toys. The air smells of fried dough. Neon flashes red and green. Someone passes me in a Blue Lives Matter T-shirt.

I watch the fireworks with a neighbor in the fire department, a retired earth sciences teacher. Red sparks bloom overhead. I ask about joining the fire department. Explosions dazzle against the darkness.

Why do you want to join? The teacher yells over the noise. The shriek of roman candles makes any answer impossible. I say something about sirens and guilt, knowing someone else is waking at 3:37 or 4:53 for their neighbors, for me, and now that my parents are dead I have time to.

I also want to mention the floods we get, and the logger's death. His body had to be recovered by his uncle and cousin in the department. I cannot imagine that pain.

The words drift. Bursts of blue and white gleam off the faces of the crowd around us.

What I don't say or can't explain is that joining is to say I am here and serve, but there's also politics in the alarms and emergencies and political urgency. Everything feels torn between us and them whatever *us* we are, and the fire department is full of older white men, good-old boys who might not associate the red in redneck with miners, strikes and links to Wobblies and communists. There are my parents, too, my dad with the broom and my mom with the cat. Joining is about a transcendence I want to achieve, to be all of us, all together. That too feels political in a small town where the volunteer fire department is the most basic civic institution. It is our mutual aid society.

In the now of writing, I also have time—not just free time but other times.

———

That summer, the president says he will restore law and order, and we're just getting started. He says your Second Amendment is safe. He makes this speech in a town with a Lenape name. Soon he calls racists fine people.

At the picnic in the woods, alcohol is passed man to man and boy to boy. Exhaustion transforms into a jangly feel in their bones of the fight to come that day. At this table I see Brisbane and Zera Preston and Bluebeard, even Devyr, though surely he is in Albany this day. He comes often though to the Catskills to meet with farmers, and I imagine his sitting down with the men in their masks.

In these days of summer, one August transposes into another. It is early in the month: a slim moon in the night sky. The men travel in wagons, driving twenty miles in the dark and at dawn. If asked, they say they're off fishing, but they carry no poles, no fishing gear. They stop for whiskey and drink and sleep in a barn. In the morning the farmer serves them breakfast and joins them with his cart. Guns are hidden under blankets. Dresses are wrapped in parcels. A man, Gus, meets them on my hill. All have fake names like Bullet Hawk and Hawk Anteluba, Red Bird and Rainbow.

I see the smudged ink on the Leatherheads' letter, like blood.

In both Augusts, men carry dirks, knives, guns, swords, torches . . . The day after those fine people rally around a racist monument in Charlottesville and march with tiki torches and murder a woman, running her over with a car, I stand at the gates of my county fair. I shake fists and signs. The fair will not stop selling or displaying the Confederate flag. I lunge at the fair commissioner. Cops circle. Rudd's brother Burr gives a speech in protest. We reap what we sow, he says. He talks about family: Revolution and Civil War, code words and dog whistles. We rally in front of the fair's gates. Rage shudders through my body. Anger has a taste and smell: coins and sweat, something wiry and silver. I yell. Burr speaks, and in this time, these times, both times, that time is now. The us, the we. Violence shimmers like a mirage.

Burr mentions the relatives who fought, and the cops are on all sides, and in another world, this different August, they are amassed on a hillside in Andes, just west of my town. Cut to that other August: a cop is shot. Lines are drawn on the land.

—

My picture ends up in the local paper. I'm thrusting a sign in the air. That week at the dump, the guys working there, of whom I am fond, teasingly call me Trouble. Here comes Trouble, they say.

—

The cop is the enemy, Osman Steele. A portrait of him hangs in an old tavern that serves as the Andes historical society. It was painted maybe a year before his death, and he has an imperious expression: long nose and sleepy eyes and wears something like a cravat. Turned to the side, he looks down at the painter, or at us. The Anti-Renters call the officials "foxes." He has red hair. *Make your red hair redder.*

—

In the paper I'm wearing cut-offs and anger. My sign is aloft, my mouth caught in a jeer.

Now a road sign at the entrance to Andes is emblazoned with one of Steele's taunts: "Lead can't penetrate Steele." He makes the boast the morning he heads to Moses Earle's farm, August 7, 1845. He's in this very tavern drinking, and the owner warns him not to go.

At the dump one of the men stands with me as I hold a carton of recycling. I saw you in the paper, Trouble, he says. His voice: levity, joking, and I could laugh and shrug. I don't know what to say. He's a walrus of a man with a Tom Selleck mustache and wire-frame glasses. And, I have stood here before and asked if I could hang out with them for the day. I have an affinity for the dump, for the artistry of the two men who work here, both, in fact, walruses of men with Tom Selleck mustaches. The one I'm speaking with now has told me about his collection of glass insulator caps from power lines and telephone poles, and how he wants one from England, and we have talked about the installations he makes from things people throw out: the TVs stacked on high, the group of mannequins including a child in an orange safety vest, the yard figurines and statues of dogs, cats, horses, roosters, rabbits, and other assorted animals on a ledge above the men's office. Nearby a plastic buck once used for target practice is surrounded by plastic flowers. He has told me about the deer he sees around the transfer station and the turkeys that browse on the hill, and I have asked if he's been out hunting yet that year. He has said no, I don't hunt, not anymore. And I have told him that's a shame and he has said, Nah, I just can't, can't bear to; by which I understand that he just doesn't have the heart for it, not any longer.

We have had, I guess, more than small talk but I am nervous to answer and I look into my plastic bin: the mayo jar with its blue lid and an empty bottle of cheap rosé, organic peanut butter—more than one container of organic peanut butter—and another of tahini and an olive oil bottle to which a golden slick of oil clings, and I feel put on the spot by my stuff; it marks me out. No time has passed. And, it feels like centuries. On the ground broken glass coruscates in the light. I have to say something, and the sun is on my calves, and I say I don't know.

At my feet the glass twinkles and taunts. I glance at him and the glue where the label had been on the mayo jar. I must explain this August.

Free and fair for all, I say, as if some libertarian line. I don't know about you, but I live here to be free, to be in the country, to lead life as I want—and I look again at mayo, the glue, and a red dribble of wine that has stained the bin—And, if I moved here to be free and that flag is definitely not freedom—if it's only free for some or fair for few, I don't want that. I evade mentioning my family, my Black cousins and my own connections. I flush. Someone tosses recycling into the canisters, glass shatters behind us. A pickup pulls in, and to my relief the walrus of a man with his wire-frame glasses says, Yeah, that makes sense. I get that.

Chapter 19

THE DAY WE MOVE INTO the new house, David touches each thing—my mother's rocker, the one she'd once held me in; the dining room table; a pillow—as if to reassure himself he is here, or they are. It reminds me of a gesture she made one afternoon when we brought her home from the hospital.

In the morning we wake up, and here is this view, impossible green, a ridgeline and the sky an endless azure. I think this is what wealthy people pay for: views onto nothing. But, it is not nothing. There is also Clum and Kittle and my parents. If my mom had not died, though, we would have lost the house and the land. These objects, and this house, are recreations holding emotional weight, and I do not feel round but flat here.

—

David comes home one afternoon to find a turtle's nest that a mason accidentally crushed. He was moving a piece of bluestone, and the turtle has laid her eggs in the soil that was leveled a couple days before.

David stares at the dirt. Stone dust, grit, and soil are churned up. White, leathery eggs are broken and bloody. He doesn't say anything. The builder apologizes over and over. He leaves and still David stares. The eggs are a snapping turtle's, and we can't count them. Or don't. A turtle will lay dozens, often forty or more in a clutch, and they are often eaten by foxes and herons or crows. The ones that survive, though, can live for decades.

The nest's very existence is ineffable. Turtles will dig trial holes before choosing where to lay their eggs. The nest is always the same shape, like a bottle, with the same sun exposure. The temperature has to be precise, and often hatchlings will overwinter underground. Nearby we will find a wren's nest woven with a snake's shed skin to ward off predators, and on a light fixture a phoebe makes a nest. It is beautiful, built of moss and dried grass. White strands of fur line the center. How did she gather the fur? Did she find it on the ground? Was it from a deer, a coyote?

How do they know all of this?

———

David will tell me that he needs to quit his job. He will say he does not know how to quit, he will say he cannot keep doing it. He will say he doesn't know how not to do it. He will list all the work he has done in his life, washing dishes, serving drinks to American tourists searching for Shakespeare and ye olde London, working in a grocery store that sold only packaged frozen food, working in an artificial limb factory, working to destroy faulty gas masks for the British Ministry of Defense, then working on a production line for the Ministry of Defense, quitting the production line, and then working for the past two decades as a designer. He will list the awards he has been given. He will tell me what his last client said to him, words that cut him to the quick. What do I do, he asks. He does not want an answer. I try to give a dozen different answers, all of them trying to help. None of them help. And for him to even be able to ask that question, to get to that question, takes him the many miles that we have walked up Pakatakan this day.

———

The dose of the pistols comes at last. Devyr has suggested organizing bands in small cells of ten men, known only to their leader, which sounds like a terrorist cell. It is a summer of droughts, it is two summers of droughts; it is this year; it is 1845, the Eighth Moon.

———

August, not September. The gentian blooms, with its bitter draft, and in the crime novel that tries to connect to the land, the gun goes off.

Someone trenches an electric line to the new house. I take a picture of the woman driving the backhoe to post to Facebook, only she's disappeared from the site. I ask why, and she says—It's all too crazy, too much, with all the politics and people going off on this and that.

I nod vaguely. I get that. She says something about protests and people and everyone burning stuff up, their neighborhoods up, and how all lives matter. I am stunned and silent and stumble to say something about rage in the face of injustices and poverty and being shot by cops, and what do you do if you feel like your life is worthless?

She says, "Look at us here, we're not heard. No one listens to us. There's poverty and no help and it's not getting any better, and we don't burn stuff up."

But they do, they did.

The water cop says:
There's this idea that rural America is an upstanding way of life, and politicians feed off paranoia and anger. They should really fear the expansion of people thinking because that's how revolutions start. I think armed revolution is the key, and politicians should fear people getting together.

There's the farmer up the road from me who is mortgaged to the hilt. Milk prices continue to plunge. There's the logger who talked of the $900 shoes and died in a farming accident. In the tent the birds have stopped singing and the blackberries are fruiting with their iron-red juices.

And, there are my students with their debt and the unanswerable question about fighting that still hangs in the air for me.

—

That summer of 1845, someone reports at one protest, "As many as 200 indians and 4- or 500 pale faces come out." Five thousand at another. Bullet box or ballot box. Moses Earle, Steve's relation, owes sixty-four dollars in rent, about two thousand dollars today. The lease has its language about distrain and distress. Earle is about to suffer this distress. The sheriff tries to collect twice what he owes. The sale of Earle's assets, his animals, the only things he has of any real value, is set for July twenty-ninth. Hundreds of Calico Indians show up high on Dingle Hill, the ridge where Earle farms. The auction is postponed until August seventh at 1 p.m. The day before, the *Albany*

Freeholder publishes "The Contest" by the anonymous bard of Middletown:

> When you hear the trumpet sound,
> Foremost in your ranks be found;
> Crush oppression to the ground—
> Set the helpless free.

Those men in their dresses in the wagon, with the fishing and the drinking, the dirks and knives, guns, axes, and tomahawks and the torches, these men it is terrifying to meet on the street, in the road, head to Earle's farm twenty miles away.

That night the only light is a thin sliver of the waxing moon. Warren Scudder, Bluebeard, heads up the group. They hail from Gould's town, Roxbury, and ride over in the cart belonging to Scudder's father, the Baptist minister. Their disguises and weapons are concealed in the wagon. They stop at a tavern and buy a half gallon of whiskey—these Baptists aren't supposed to drink. They get food and more drink somewhere else. Someone, a farmer, tells them the easiest way to Earle's is over Hubbell Hill to my hill and my road. They "staid the night" at a Sanford farm just up from me. Sanfords are still there, including Shirley, Muriel's best friend from childhood.

Someone else in Scudder's group, Zera Preston, recounts that at the Sanfords', "They got us breakfast did not pay anything." I see him skinny and angry in his baggy calico dress as he takes up with grown men full of righteous rage. He says two other boys meet up with them. How old can they be when this child himself calls them "boys"? Another person traveling with them recounts having a drink in the barn before leaving, and when they do, Gus, Augustus Kittle, comes too.

———

Faces are aglitter in the light of burning torches.

Men in costumes, men in khakis and white shirts, a uniform of whiteness, a flag wrapped around a man's naked torso; another draped in black, the flash on a screen as crowds storm forward. The thud of bodies, the chants, the yells, *No KKK; no fascist USA.* A skyscraper's black façade, the lights of the city distort and bend in the plate glass windows. Above the door a single name in gold. At crash barriers people surge. *It is nothing less than a civil war.* There is a pounding of chests and painted bodies thrusting toward a camera. *Patriotism over socialism . . . I don't believe in violence but . . .* On the other side of all these conjunctions is one conclusion. One sound, a crescendo. *Hang 'em by a rope . . . I heard the breaking of glass. I called the police right away . . . I was appalled. Tires screeched. Assaulting our people your days are numbered. The American people are rising against you. I'm ready to bleed.*

A man in his grasping at love and hate cheers him on. The man says, yes, I'm ready to bleed. A man in a white T-shirt draws a sword and holds it over his head. Whose streets? Our streets. Resistance is necessary. Cops in a line, legs spread, arms crossed. Don't cross. Shields up and visors down. Their faces impenetrable; their lines a deployment, a battle formation, war. In a park under a marble arch celebrating George Washington and national triumph, a man taunts me. I teach two blocks away. The cops are impassive. An electric current courses through my body. A friend grabs my arm: Don't fight. She hurries me off. Don't engage. Don't say anything. He's here to provoke you. He's been paid to do this.

———

Warren Scudder announces: "The first man who bid on the property would be death to him. Cattle would not be shot." The implication: people will be. The group is drunk by the time they reach Moses Earle's on Dingle Hill. Other Calico Indians appear at his farmhouse for breakfast. Women have come to cook for them. This morning on the mountain in the meadows, in the long grass, the Calico Indians gather. They clutch bundles under their arms, crossing fields as if to work. The bundles contain dresses and masks. A hundred and thirty of them come, one man guesses; two hundred, another says; and a third reckons five hundred. Also on hand are dozens of "pale faces," as civilian sympathizers and organizers are called, those who don't don disguises.

One is William Brisbane, the recent Scottish immigrant. At a meeting at Earle's house the week before, he argued that paying Earle's rent was untenable if they're trying to protest all rent. "Hypocrisy" is the word he uses. On the way to his farm today Brisbane passes someone singing "an old country song" about enlisting.

I find the lyrics and guess how they must have been changed.

> Our 'prentice Tom may now refuse
> To wipe his scoundrel Master's Shoes,

For now he's free to sing and play
Over the Hills and far away.
Over the Hills and O'er the Main,
To Flanders, Portugal, and Spain,
The sheriff commands and we'll nay obey
Over the Hills and far away.

Courage, boys, 'tis one to ten,
But we return all gentlemen
While conquering colors we display,
Over the hills and far away.
Over the Hills and O'er the Main,
To Andes and Dingle Hill, we name,
The sheriff commands and we'll never obey
Over the Hills and far away.

Warren Scudder arrives and takes charge. He is thirty-three, with black hair and a red cloth mask. It's topped by a military cap. He faces off against Peter Wright, the landlord's agent. Osman Steele, the undersheriff, shows up without a posse, just his brother-in-law Constable Erastus Edgerton, whose father was threatened by the Leatherheads. The two men come, it seems, for the sport of it. On their horses, Edgerton and Steele stand ten yards from where the Calico Indians are massed.

Later, people recount the events that take place over the next half hour. How postmodern the testimony is. Like *Roshomon*, each angle a different perspective.

He ordered the peace.
His pistol was in the air.

He ordered the peace three times.

I did see a pistol in his hand. I did not see a pistol in Edgerton's hand. I did not see a pistol in Edgerton's hand go off.

Steele said I dare you to shoot my horse . . .

Edgerton said the first man that offers to stop me I will shoot him or shoot him dead.

I saw the pistol in Steele's hand before any of the firing began.

I saw Steele & Edgerton immediately draw their pistols before there was a shot fired. When Edgerton drew his pistol I have no doubt he fired—he fired then, I have no doubt of it.

I saw smoke from his pistol.

The first discharge was from his pistol.

As Steele's pistol first discharged his horse wheeled to the left.

Edgerton commands the peace.

Two flashes.

Heard two balls whistle by.

I did not expect any firing—I thought to myself there is no use of running.

It gave me terrible bad.

I saw his pistol raised—in his right hand.

I swear it is possible to see a pistol fired & see neither flash nor smoke.

After he fired there was an instantaneous discharge spat spat spat.

There was no peace elapsed between the two expressions. The crash of the guns was almost instantaneous. I thought to myself of running.

I was amazed. I stood stock still, it gave me a

terrible bad, I was very bad. 6 or 8 guns fired. The second & next time, as quick as thought, 3 or 4 guns went off. I saw E's horse down, as quick as thought.

I saw the balls.

The first guns that were fired were <u>heavy guns</u>.

I cannot say whether the report was made by a pistol, musket rifle, or shotgun; the noise was about the same sound—there were more than three shots all sounded about alike & could not have been fired by two persons.

I fled out of the bars as I heard the sound of Edgerton's pistol into the middle of the road.

Three guns were fired, loud reports: <u>that that that</u> I saw Steele fire but once.

Could not Say how many Shots were fired Thinks fifty.

I should think there were 12 Shots.

Did not see Steele, Edgerton, or Wright draw their pistol. I thought at first I heard three or four reports—I was very much frightened.

I saw the pistol in Steel's hand before any firing began; I saw smoke come out of the pistol; I saw smoke from Steel's pistol. I heard the report & it sounded a heavy report. Steele's horse was on the wheel as Steele fetched over his pistol to fire— and that is the only time I saw Steele fire.

His horse reeled up. I saw the blood come out of the fore shoulder of E's horse. I did not see the ball that passed through Steele's body. The shot I saw when his coat flew hit higher up than his bowels & both his coat flaps flew up.

His horse wheeled to the left, & as he wheeled I
saw his horse was wounded & then I saw Steele
was wounded & he pitched over forward and fell
off his horse quick as thought.

Steele was in the act of firing, his hand raised & in
the act of firing & he fell from his horse.

After that fire Steele leaned himself forward &
grasped the main & Steele's horse made three
plunges and fell. Steele fell off the third plunge.
Steele & the horse fell together. They fell at the
same time.

———

Osman Steele dies that night.

———

Like with any cop killing, the force of the law comes
down mightily and it comes down fast. A panel of judges
convenes the next day, and for the next month meets every day and on into the night, except on Sundays. The
governor declares the county in a state of insurrection.
Two hundred and forty-eight people are rounded up and
arrested. A jail is hastily erected in the square outside the
courthouse where I search these records now. At a metal
desk in a tiny room in the basement I flick through boxes
of testimony.

The air is tight and close and smells of paper dust. I read
statements about Augustus and his cousins. The young
Zera Preston, with his gluey, gummy account, refuses to
testify, as if pleading the Fifth. It's not called that in the
records, and he is brought back time and again until he

answers. Rudd's relative Harvey is arrested. I find the warrant. I have on gloves but want to touch the ink and run my fingers over letters that are hard to decipher in their formal cursive. Harvey, like Gus, is seventeen and a "laborer." Two brothers who ride with Scudder talk of drinking and driving in the carts. I read testimony from people whose families run businesses today. One testifies, "If they undertook to come out with a posse they would lose their cocanuts." I can't help but laugh at the coconuts.

There are others too in the records and still nearby. Even Kittles still live in the community. I call them to ask about Gus.

These Kittles know nothing of this Augustus.

—

Someone up my road states: "My name is Hawk Anteluba." He is a Calico Indian chief. His son admits: "I became an indian after it was illegal. My father's tribe includes Augustus Kittle."

John Van Steenburgh: "I saw Augustus Kettle mask up. Can't tell what arms.

Alexander Brush: "I became an anti-Renter for the good of my country."

Elizabeth Campbell: "We baked." Only a handful of women testify, and that's her only line.

John Davis: "I swore by the upraised hand."

Obed Hendricks: "I reside in Middletown I am a justice of the peace I bought the soil this summer. I paid 25 cents when I joined."

—

I bought the soil. For the good of my country.

Pause on the words. Time resounds through the century. In a year I will recount the testimony for Obed Hendricks's great-great-great-grandnephew. (There may be more greats- and grands in there that I've forgotten, so many of them it's impossible to keep them straight.)

Did you know, I tell him, what he, what Obed, said? My voice arcs up. We are in a trailer with the AC on. It is summer at the Fireman's Fair. Obed—I love the name and must use it as often as possible—was the justice of the peace, a man of the law, breaking the law, lined up with militants, the most militant in the country, here, here, I say, to redistribute land to redistribute wealth.

The great-great- and grand- smiles and nods. I don't mention socialism. It has taken some courage to tell him this exciting news of another era. The great-great- and grand- works for New York City, for its water that is of here and there. He asks if I have found another relative, more directly related. It turns out these Hendrickses have been here longer than just about any other white settlers. In this tiny trailer in the village park, where the fair is about to begin, this Hendricks tells me too about his father who loved history.

The fire department is about to hold a raffle in his father's name to fund a scholarship for a senior in the central school. I hand him the tickets I've sold, and the cash. In the trailer the fan kicks on, and outside we can hear the carneys setting up the rides.

I realize I have bought the soil. I've joined. I am now a member of the fire department. My sisters say our father would be proud.

I am the asthmatic firefighter, allergic to smoke. I cannot fight fires. My doctor won't allow it, and there are two things you need to join: a doctor's note and no arson convictions. Her note only allows me to do scene support and traffic direction. Turns out traffic control is one of things we do most often: at car accidents and fires and for medevac helicopters, and after the fireworks as people stream out of the fair. I am technically a "peace officer." I am called "fire police." I am a cop, and I think too of that law in 1845 and those "peace officers" who were required to arrest my neighbors in masks. Some like Obed Hendricks refused.

I learn from Rudd's brother Burr that the anti-mask law is still in effect.

Chapter 20

DAVID RETURNS FROM ANOTHER TRIP installing an exhibition he designed. A global purveyor of luxury goods holds an event in the exhibition, hoping that the guests will take photos and that their photos will feature the brand, and then the photos and brand will flit and float on a platform to get hearts and likes, thumbs-up and approval. There is a dinner. There is a movie. There is a live orchestra. David is told to stay in the kitchen. David has done the burnishing and polishing of corporate interests. He says he is done with this burnishing and polishing.

A notice is posted at the robber baron swimming pool. They need volunteers. They need board members. David volunteers.

August 2018: My first meeting at the fire department. Men wander in dressed in T-shirts and shorts, nearly everyone wearing at least one garment emblazoned with the department's Maltese cross logo. A neighbor cooks for us. Folding tables are laid out with chips, dips, crackers, crudités of cut carrots and celery.

Stacking chairs are arranged in a square, and we all face the flag. The meeting begins with the Pledge of Allegiance. A moment of shock hangs suspended as I realize I have to say this oath that I've not repeated since sixth grade. The men around me put their hands on their chests, and I see that I too must put a hand to my heart and declare fealty, here in a country, our country, that does not feel united, where inequality makes union an impossibility. And, we say in this language I also find impossible: "One nation under God." I think which god? Which god would allow such injustice?

My inner monologue goes on with the flag in the corner, the plaques on the wall, the men and their hats off, these ball caps sporting the names of chainsaw companies and tractor suppliers, and to my right is Obed Hendricks's great-great- and grand-, and to my left is the retired teacher who I asked about joining, who has said, "Of course, you can do it." At my interview where I have to attest to the fact that I have no arson convictions, Obed's great-great- too says, "Of course you can do it." And so they say join, and I do join, and now they all look at the flag in the corner, and it comes to us saying, "And liberty and justice for all." I yearn for it to be true. I hear the chorus of the men's voices and the two other women in the room—one whose father is now the village mayor. She has been in the department since she was in high school—she is a Hubbell. On the wall the medals and plaques gleam, and the photos of men in uniforms all watch us, and I look again at the flag. At the top of the flagpole is an eagle with arrows. The eagle and arrows are a symbol of the Haudenosaunee's linked confederacy, adopted by the United States to represent ours.

After the meeting, after I am welcomed to the department, after there has been applause, after names are read out for who must stay behind to clean up—including the newest recruit—after we approve the budget and hear the treasurer's report and the number of emergency calls last month, and hear about the success of this year's carnival, we eat dinner together. The dinner is franks and beans. A vegetarian option is provided. (Some of us, it turns out, are vegetarians.) And, at the round folding tables with the stacking chairs, I drink a Michelob Ultra and poke at my food. There is sheet cake for desert, and small talk I do not know how to make. It is of weather, of heat and droughts and ponds and mowing. I feel my insides tighten, my grin stiffen. This is how not fitting in feels. I wonder about my dad and all the trips to rural co-ops he made, all the people he met and dinners he ate and how he could fit in. In her moments of generosity my mother would say that this was his gift. The beer can in my palm grows warm.

———

William Brisbane, the Scottish immigrant, carries Osman Steele's body into Moses Earle's home. He prepares a bed for him; he cries when the man dies.

Brisbane is new here. I see him in my mind. He is thirty three, nearly my age when I moved. He must have fled tenancy in Scotland, then he speaks up against rent but works as a subtenant on a rented farm. On the fourth of July 1844 when he has been in the United States for five years and in Andes for four, he declares, "The Earth is as free for man to enjoy as the air & that no man has a right to appropriate it to himself any more than he can cultivate it with his own hands."

Those words are a threshold. He came here for equal justice, for all, for a belief in liberty that leads him to speak out, and every time I cross his words, I pause to reorder their meaning. Sometimes I hear my dad, where he believes in shared resources, the public good. Other times

I wonder whom that freedom extends to? Which man or men are included in the statement about enjoying the air? But, mostly in his words I hold onto the idea that Brisbane, a spokesman for the Anti-Renters, believes no one should own the land, that it is a common good and communal. And, this is what I want to hold onto. It is for us, all of us to share, all together.

———

There is also how Brisbane the newcomer speaks up, but in the fire department where families have served for generations and membership comes with rules I do not understand, I am silent. I feel lost and out of place.

———

It is nearly four years after the election for Hope when David becomes a citizen. Before that, he never protested, was scared even of speeding tickets and making mistakes on his taxes. For the citizenship exam he spends weeks studying, which requires driving miles in the car. The test has one hundred questions only available on a CD, and the only CD player is in the car. So, he drives over mountains, circles the reservoir, sometimes parks and stares at the water just to listen to a woman's neutral voice ask: *What is the supreme law of the land?*
Or:

What is the economic system in the United States?
- *capitalist economy*
- *market economy*

The idea of self-government is in the first three words of the Constitution. What are these words?
- *We the People*

What is <u>one</u> right or freedom from the First Amendment?
Another question: **name one American Indian tribe in the United States.** None of the answers include the Lenape, whose land we live on.

At the ceremony in Binghamton, everyone claps and cries, even the judge. It is this moment of all of us together. She says this is her greatest honor as a jurist. She calls out the names of each new citizen, all forty-nine of them, and the country from which they have emigrated. We in the audience, friends and family members in our best suits and dresses, applaud. We cheer the loudest for those who have come the furthest, from the most troubled countries, ones with which we are at war, or perceived war; ones that require the most perseverance to get here. Unlike on the news, these people are heroes this day in this courtroom in this rust belt town. Together we repeat the Pledge of Allegiance and clap.

All three of them, Brisbane, Devyr, and David have left Britain, David only coming for my health. And, Brisbane and Devyr are maybe not even citizens when they organize the Anti-Renters, but the men talk of "us" and are committed to liberty, to this "for all." They are also committed to this war. David who has come for my health, has also found the place he belongs.

—

He goes out with his chainsaw to cut wood for next winter. Days shorten; dawn looks like dusk. We wake in the dark. Over a saddle in the ridge, the sun rises, glistening.

Rudd once told us it would come up there in fall and winter. David works slowly, methodically with the HELPP, which demands attention to hinges and plans.

His job delivers an ultimatum: he must move back to the UK or resign.

———

The posse comes for Brisbane in mid-August, a week after the murder. He calls to his wife, and later he writes in a letter, "Their bayonets glittered in the setting sun."

They glint for me into this moment, sparking and flashing.

Many have fled, run to the hills and hollows, caves and Canada. Few are left to carry in the crops, and soon winter will come early, with snow in September. There will be starvation and privation for these people who are already poor. And, Brisbane is in the hayfield with his wife. There are no threshing machines, nothing to make this labor easier. He yells to her. Janet is her name. "Jenny!" he calls her, my name. He calls me.

———

Next: he's dragged off on a horse he calls, "a tumble-down kind of a machine . . . so extremely lame" that it sounds like it's calling out "Down with rent! Down with rent!" which is the only way he can abide this injustice. In jail, the "Delhi Bastille," he says, "by some strange sort of legerdemain I had become an American Robin Hood." Steal from the rich, give to the poor.

To think of this man in his early thirties, with eight kids, the youngest only two months old, is already to conjure a life so far away from mine it's nearly impossible. Just to imagine crossing from Scotland: the boat, being stuck in steerage, seasickness and disease and countless other details omitted where death is your companion. To come here for some image of freedom, to find that it is not free and definitely not for all. To work the soil—the two rocks for every dirt—and to declare I bought the soil, to join his neighbors in their struggle and their rent strike. And, through this all to have humor. That is what gets me.

I find a picture of him taken thirty years later. His eyes are wide and round, his face long and pinched. He has a beard—the sort men wore then, without a mustache. It makes his face look bald and embarrassing, like some decorative fringe has been tacked on around the chin. Still, there's a smile. It's sly; maybe he's trying to swallow or stifle it. In photographs at the time you're supposed to be grave, and he cannot even manage that. His wit twinkles through, just like with all these moments in jail. He is also a man who can cry. In jail he says, "I never knew before I was somebody."

———

August twenty-first, neighbors on my road are hauled in for questioning. These are the people who might have had a small role, who maybe gave the Calico Indians some assistance. One elderly man Salman Beeman born a year before the Revolution, and who fought in the War of 1812, is dragged before the panel of judges that morning. His words ring with indignation. His statement is three lines long: "Beeman Hill in Middletown was named after me—I follow farming I own a farm 82 acres, soil farm I have one grandson—he quit them last . . ." The rest is not recorded. My guess is his grandson quit the rebels the last winter or spring, some earlier season. For his part, Rudd's relative says he's given four dollars to the Anti-Rent association.

The indictments that follow string out a litany of names. One lists Augustus Kittle, his cousins, and Warren Scudder and Zera Preston who:

> With force & arms unlawfully wickedly willfully
> feloniously riotously & tumultuously did assem-
> ble & gather together to disturb the peace of the
> people of the state of New York & did then &
> there paint discolour cover & conceal their & each
> of their faces and did so disguise their & each of
> their faces persons as to prevent themselves from
> being identified & did then & there arm them-
> selves with swords dirks guns rifles pistols &
> other offensive weapons & while so having their
> & each of their faces painted discoloured, covered
> & concealed & their & each of their persons do

disguised as aforesaid & being so then & there unlawfully riotously & feloniously assembled & gathered together as aforesaid & being so armed with swords dirks guns rifles pistols & other offensive weapons did then & there make great noise riot tumult & disturbance for a long space of time to wit for the space of one hour then next ensuing to the great terror and disturbance not only of the good people then & there inhabiting, residing & being but of all other good people of the state of New York then & there passing and repassing along the public streets & highways in contempt of the said people & their laws and contrary to the provisions of the act entitled "An act to prevent persons appearing disguised & armed" passed January 28, 1845 against the form of the statute & of said act in such case made & provided & against the peace of the people of the state of New York & their dignity—

And, that's not even all of it. The long lines of adjectives and adverbs, that "unlawfully wickedly willfully feloniously riotously & tumultuously," without any commas, could almost be funny. Another charge accuses Kittle of being disguised "to the evil example of all others." The only names that don't appear in the arrests in 1845: Peter and his son John Clum.

I wonder what the two of them felt that night as Kittle and Scudder and Preston headed to Moses Earle's, what they heard down on the road, what had come up over the valley, and what it's like to know your neighbors are willing to go to prison and sacrifice everything for you?

—

This morning in the tent next to David, I stare outside as a fog lifts, and we are a hundred feet from Clum's house. Pearly everlastings have bloomed and dried into a perfect version of the tiny white flower. I drag him out early with barely any coffee and no breakfast to protect the gentians from the deer. We go down the hill toting an old plastic milk jug filled with homemade deer repellant (curdled milk, rotten eggs, garlic, and red pepper). He says something about what a cop I am now, wielding pepper spray against deer. We also clutch metal cages, something like tomato cages, to put around the plants. He says something too about ICE. I tell him the gentians are nearly endangered. But he is also happy to help. He gathers one up, holding the stems and glossy leaves gently as I put the stakes around. In the tent I've asked him to read over this manuscript. He glances up. He has surveyors' tape in his hands to fix to the fence so the deer can see it. He worries they might hurt themselves.

He says, It's strange reading about yourself.

Are you okay with it? I curve my voice around the words hoping to soften whatever edges he's found.

It's not wrong, he says. Just, you hope not to be too stupid or awful.

Of course he is flattened.

—

As the gentians bloom, their leaves grow purple like the flower. Now they are starting to brown. Two different kinds of closed gentians, bottle gentians, grow in the Northeast. Ours is *andrewsii*, Andrew's gentian, named for a British botanist who died in 1830 and never came to the United States. I read that the Haudenosaunee have used the plant as an analgesic for pain and headaches but also as a cure for lonesomeness. This ethnobotany is cold and clinical, listing symptoms and treatments, but I appreciate this closed flower being adopted for loneliness. I try to picture Peter Clum and his consumption, dying in the small, damp shack no bigger than eight-by-ten feet across. One of the things my mom would complain about with my father was that he hiked too fast in Vermont. She would list all the things he didn't see—the ferns and flowers and her.

Nearby, a couple of ancient apple trees grow. Their limbs decay; some have fallen to the ground. One trunk is split, and lichen grows on the bark. A forester friend tells us that the trees look to be 150 years old. The biggest has only a single branch still alive, and yet suckers of new growth reach for the sky. I realize the trees must have been planted in the Civil War, when Lincoln was a baby on the farm next door and this land was cultivated by John Clum.

David has told his job he needs to think about their request for a week. The week comes, and I have no idea what he will say. I try to follow him outside and tell him a year, that's nothing, we could go back for a year. No, no, no, he says. We sit on the stoop and face the gravel drive.

In the new house my mom, the plant, sits on the bar. My sisters discuss how this would make her happy, being at the center of things, being at the bar, maybe with some bourbon, maybe a glass of wine. The summer after we move she blooms not once but twice—bursting forth in a cluster flowers. Each is pale-pink velvet with an ivory star at the center, which looks truly like it's been carved of wax and then studded with a ruby heart.

—

In the present of writing, I think of Clum's apple tree and lichen, and lichen as a sense of time—time outside of human time. Lichens are one of the oldest organisms; some live for thousands of years. The plant—not a plant at all, it's a marriage of fungi and algae—breaks down the rocks to release the minerals, and those minerals go into the soil. There are so many apple trees here because of these minerals, because of our two rocks for every dirt.

These lichens are also a metaphor, or the metaphor by which I want to live. They are a cooperative ecosystem, fungi and algae joined as one, spreading on rocks and trees. On Clum's apple trees they spiral out in a circle called a green shield. The partners, the algae and fungi, each work together to gain water and nutrients from the atmosphere, from rain and dust. Some lichen is so sensitive to the air it breathes that climate change and increased carbon dioxide in the atmosphere threaten it. Others, the green shields, are "some of the first to recolonize areas that have experienced heavy air pollution."

The word lichen comes from the Greek, to lick. I think again, *I bought the soil*. I eat the soil through these lichen as the organism connects rocks and earth. It connects me to the ground here. The soil, the dirt—is in me; the rocks are in me; the place is part of me. Mutualism—the algae and fungi—are mutual aid for each other, for the soil, and the soil for us. In the word "soil," I also hear "social," as if they're linked inextricably.

This sense of time as being outside human time is a comfort. The dirt is a record of the centuries. The minerals in the rocks nourish microbes, microbes nourish mycelia; mycelia nourish plants. And, the soil remembers. Dig into it with a spade, you see roots tangled under the surface. It's limned with delicate fine filaments. My heart breaks, tearing into them. The ground takes years to recover. Soils hold the history of a place, and around Clum's foundations nettles and gooseberries grow. By the barn's grand stone walls, jack-in-the-pulpits spread. With their green folded hood, the flowers are hard to spot. They open like some hidden lily of the leaf litter, and the plants live for a quarter-century or more, switching sexes with age. The small blooms are male and the larger, older ones female. They eat the insects that pollinate them. They are carnivorous. I loved these spring flowers as a child and still hum a song I was taught in elementary school about them. They are nourished by the calcium in soil.

Here, with this two rocks for every dirt, in lichen time—soil time—the earth unspools in a different time. Apple trees also grow from the piles of stones John and Catherine Clum collected in the field.

After his mother dies, John Clum lives on this land in this shack/shed with his wife and thirteen children. He never owns it. He is always a tenant, always poor. Now I live just down the hill from the ruins, in the house modeled on my parents' home, and try to re-create some of their ideals. I walk through Peter and John and Jane Clum's fields. I think of them, and my mom and Muriel, and her father and my dad. The year her father's cow, Sun's Ideal, with her 13,000 pounds of milk, appears in the newspaper, my parents take over the rural co-operative two counties away.

I stare at a picture of them on a dirt road in Upstate New York.

David tells his job he will leave. He can't go back, he says. I am a citizen here. This is my home.

In this time and that time and in all these times, there is also love—or I want there to be, the tender flowers of the anarchist Haymarket trial plus Brisbane's humor and my parents smiling outside the co-op, my mom in her bobby socks and my dad with a broom, and Brisbane saying, "I never knew before I was somebody" and realizing his importance. There is the judge and people crying and welcoming new citizens into something the judge calls the American experiment.

In all the anger and ire, this is what I am missing: the love that mutualism requires, the care, the self-sacrifice. Love is part of that transcendence in the "Hello Stranger Put Your Loving Hand in Mine." It is about this place and time and the slipstream, on one side of which is chaos in both of these Augusts of anger.

On August 16, 1845, a week after Osman Steele's death, Devyr publishes in his paper the next line from Leviticus just after the land is mine. "Ye are strangers and sojourners with me." That is, we are strangers and sojourners together.

———

One night at home in Virginia with my mother, six months before she dies, we fall into a silence. I am again in her rocker, she in the easy chair with all the books stacked by its side. There's the reading for her two book clubs and the titles she has my sisters fetch from the library. She says something about Arlington. My father is in Arlington Cemetery in what she calls the marble condo, where his ashes are interred. For years she has said she doesn't want to be there with him, and now she says she does. She says she forgives him, that she loves him.

Love, she says, we had love, and I am proud of our lives, of what we did, of you three daughters we raised, the women you've become—and all the work on co-ops, that we, he and I, did. And I see now it was the two of us all along. We built that together.

———

After she dies I find a list of all the books she's read since sometime in 1965, every single one, every single year. The year I'm born there are twenty-six, one every other week. Among them: André Gide's *Strait Is the Gate* and William Styron's *Confessions of Nat Turner*. There is also Agatha Christie's *Endless Night*. That comes almost halfway through the list at number ten, and I imagine her reading it in July in the rocking chair. I imagine the book giving her some comfort that dark summer. The first lines read: *"In my end is my beginning . . . Is there ever any particular spot where one can put one's finger and say: 'It all began that day, at such a time and such a place, with such an incident'?"*

———

I walk with my neighbor Amy up to the shack/shed, to the ruins. She's my closest friend nearby, and she will pray over something that troubles me, work or writing, or if David or I get sick. She closes her emails "God bless." I sign mine off "Much love," and I do love her deeply. Up the hill we go. Picture her: long skirts, like on the prairie, and hiking books, her hair tied up on her head. She asks about the strange cages in the field and what I'm growing. I worry she thinks it's pot and tell her about the gentians. When we reach the barn's monumental foundation, she

says, Goodness that work, those boulders, and mentions
something of providence. She tells me that back then, older
children would often sleep in the barn with the animals if
there wasn't enough space in the house.

We clamber down to the mill, the waterfalls. She asks
me to do a homeschooling project with her son and daughter on the Anti-Rent War. I'm grateful she lets me talk
about rural socialism and how our neighbors stood against
injustices we still fight today. I tell them about Augustus
and Lincoln Kittle and the Clums and Karl Marx.

I ask the children to imagine the need to take up
arms. Their homework is to design a costume for their
cause. What would you fight for? I say. Amy's son jumps
up: Drugs! I'd stop drug dealers.

He clutches the drawing of his disguise. It includes
a stockpot for a helmet. I nod warily. I tell him the pot/
helmet is great, and it is. It is breathtakingly rendered
in fine lines, but I also picture our town and county and
neighbors criminalized and how the war on drugs targets
poor people of color. Later, he gives me a watercolor of a
Calico Indian. "Ghosts on the land," he writes beneath the
image. It still hangs on the fridge.

———

In prison, in the hastily constructed jail in Delhi, Brisbane
is threatened with hanging for being a "foreign bastard."
He leaves blanks in his letter to avoid swearing in print,
but like a game of hangman, I fill in the letters. "A dap-
per stranger," he writes, comes and threatens to scatter his
family like ashes. "You are poor," the man says.

———

Structure fire at 2:33 in the morning. My job is to close the road two miles down. I stand at this intersection of some-where and nowhere, by a trailer. It's not even a double-wide, nothing that substantial, but a rusting camper with its wheels on blocks. In the kitchen the light is on, creating a sulfurous glow like *Nighthawks* in the sticks. The air is lambent and still and the stars above spin out across the sky. I feel like my job is watching this kitchen from the street, to cast a web of protection. Someone calls from a house behind me, "Where's the fire?" and my radio crack-les in the silence. I wonder if the voice behind me is the radio or god. The voice again: "Is it the Jankowsky's place?"

—

Brisbane is the one who comes for me that night, whose breath and words I know. He talks to me, and I pace back and forth on this corner and we are there together. His humor and my anger, his tears and his pleas, my father, him, the public, this promise of being free. His letters, his Jenny . . .

David, who has held my anguish, makes me coffee as I leave for the structure fire. He makes more when I return at 5 a.m.

To join is to try to transcend together. Rudd tells me he's proud of my serving in the fire department. I think it's great your joining up, someone like you. His "someone" takes in that I'm not from here, and I'm a writer, and my politics. We stand at a chicken barbecue in the grocery store park-ing lot for a family who lost their home in a fire. Rudd has been grilling. He and his brothers always show up grilling chicken halves and wholes with two sides to raise money after a crisis. He hands his friend Scott the tongs and hugs me. I kick at some dirt. I tell him that I'm awful at the job. What is unsaid is how I often don't know what to do and feel awkward in that room with the men who are all from here, who speak in a code I do not know, and that I am too nervous to ask for help or to draw attention to myself, or to say when I disagree.

Chapter 21

WE, YOU AND I, WALK up to the end of my dead-end road, and it is not dead at all. We slip past the gate of the Sanford farm where Warren Scudder "staid the night." An old track is all that's left of his path. It passes over top of Hubbell Hill, and branches and twigs crackle underfoot. It's autumn now. We follow the route Scudder took with Zera Preston before they meet up with Augustus Kittle. Leaves rustle, and I have that feeling of being porous to the world. It comes with that frisson of danger, of being alone in the woods, but we are not alone.

We cross through the forest and come out on the other side on a paved road named for Rudd's family. It's dotted with vacation homes and views of mountains majesty. Back in 1845 farms and fields would have continued forever. The trees were disappearing. Now they return, taking over old fields with scrubby maple and aspen. I study the map from 1869. I have two maps, one with the road Scudder drives and another where it has vanished, and so has he, largely. We cross this divide in two moments, ones that have bent toward the other.

My neighbors were and are the poor white people oppressed by elites often based in the city. They also tied their oppression to others, supporting abolition and suffrage. They are like Trump's supporters and are socialists like me, believing not in *I*, but *us*, a coalition together. And, they are also militant. I get caught on these contradictions. How do I bridge that distance?

The poet Lisa Robertson writes, "If I could open the temporality in sentences perhaps a transformation could take hold." I try, yet all of my questions about violence and democracy collect on the page. There's the testimony—half a gallon of whisky, drinking in the barn, the "kind of musket," Scudder's red face and red mask, and the thud, pummel, and pound, bodies and brutality, fists on flesh. *The . . . The chief drew a pistol. You'll chew something harder. I will shoot any one. Spat, spat, spat. It gave me terrible bad. His coat flaps flew up. They fell.*

Chants rise up. Time bleeds. On TV in September 2016 or August 2017 or January 2021 commentators ask, How could this happen? This is unprecedented. This is not us, not our democracy.

But it is. Under majority rule some are always tamped down, and I see wars: strikes and Pinkertons in the 1870s and 80s, that anarchist trial in the *New York Times* in 1886, the Anti-Rent War, John Brown, Bleeding Kansas, Civil Rights, fighting against men armed with guns and hoses who represent the state—the law. Taking over the wildlife refuge, the Malheur, those bad feelings rising. Those men with their long arms in the Oregon desert still say *the land is mine*. These civil wars are our wars, and I am pretty sure right now we are in a war.

These wars seem inevitable because capitalism requires inequality. The transcendence I am looking for cuts across boundaries to build class solidarity, two words that here sound stiff and stolid, but this is the us, the we, I crave.

That war and those politics bend to this time, or my

time is here, now, and then. I keep thinking of "opening the temporality and a transformation taking hold." I want to defy time in writing. Linear time, though, is always inscribed in sentences with their beginning, middle, and end. Progress is inherent in the very act of reading, and narrative plot creates a fiction of resolution happening through the steady unfolding of time. That's part of what Hardwick dispensed with in *Sleepless Nights*. The idea of progress, though, means we leave the past behind, and we get to believe the future is ever better. It is ordained.

At the same time Hardwick writes her novel in the 1970s, the socialist historian Lawrence Goodwyn is working on a book on radical rural movements. He describes how the inexorable nature of moral and economic progress stifles how we look at collectivism and leads, he puts it, to "resignation." Progress undermines radical histories. They always fail as if there are winners and losers and those pasts are over. As if those movements are not present here all along.

To reconsider time is to write against this. Without linear time, those revolutions are alive. They all offer propositions that are unfinished and here for us to take up. They cut across these years, and we can gather them together. They are each imperfect too, and, for sure, I am. I've always thought of myself as a bad socialist because I haven't known how to live as one, or how to create change, and I've turned to the past seeking answers. Now I want to lay all time together to exist in it all at once.

———

One friend, a novelist, tells me to keep moving forward in my writing. Don't go back, she says. Another friend says that nuance escapes the writer. It certainly does me. My poet friend has told me to cut the interstitials—the elements that connect the paragraphs, like time. I have and found it liberating.

Hardwick told one of her students, "Nothing is worse than a transition." She writes too in an essay on essays that they have "freedoms not so much exercised as seized." She has been with me on those cards on the wall, and in this essay of hers on essays, she says something about narrators and characters in novels today, her today being nearly a half-century ago. She explains that we need a "first-person narrator" because the "contemporary psyche" isn't "a lump of traits so much as a mist of inconsistencies." We need someone, she writes, to say, "'It seemed to me,'" rather than "'It was.'"

This is how it seems to me.

———

Writing here without the transitions, I realize everything is connected, and all of this is interstitial—marginal—about those out of time, those forgotten by time. It's the *and* and *and* and *and* of parataxis, where everything is interconnected. How could I have seen that I'd move to Margaretville in 2006 and live with a connection to 1845, to another time, to Muriel and Brisbane both as relatives and relatives in the soil?

In 1845 Brisbane and a half dozen others including Moses Earle are sent to Dannemora just as the prison opens. It's still a maximum security facility today, and there he and the other Anti-Rent convicts build the jail around themselves. No one knows who shot Steele, certainly no one admits to the crime, but two are convicted of murder. At his sentencing, one of them calls out, "Remember, my friends, I die an innocent man." In prison he writes his family:

> O! parents dear I little thought that this would be my lot
> I fear I'll die a shameful death and be my man forgot . . .
> Keep these lines remember me
> I did for friends and liberty.

After he is free, Moses Earle builds stone walls, as if he is still building the prison around himself. His own farmhouse is long gone now, but these walls remain, still snaking up the hill.

Others move west. Many leave, the land empties. William Brisbane goes to Wisconsin and later Minnesota, where that picture of him with his wry smile is taken.

And, the Calico Indians get the land. They have to buy it, though. The landlords start selling off their parcels. In the 1850 Census I find names of property owners that I've seen in arrest records. I have no idea how they scrape together the money. Maybe sympathetic neighbors help? I'm pretty sure that Kittle's three deeds are tied to a mortgage.

Soon New York State outlaws sales for distrain and distress, and politicians start talking of land and injustice. They take up the Anti-Renters' arguments and create the Free Soil Party. In 1854 the Republican Party is formed in Ripon, Wisconsin, where Brisbane had moved five years before. The town is on the site of a former Fourierist phalanx. Here, the party supports a broad coalition of special interests: abolitionists, suffragettes, Fourierists, Anti-Rent organizers, and Free Soilers. This free soil, land to whoever works it, becomes the Homestead Act, passed in the middle of the Civil War. Any settler, which is really any white settler, who goes west gets 160 acres.

And yet.

The National Reform Association has dreamt of a collective shared utopia. Instead of redistributing land into private hands and breaking feudalism, US policy is tied to so-called public land—western lands, ones that seem easy to give away. Those lands are under the government's control because they've been stolen from Indigenous Americans. That is also my neighbors' legacy. In the Anti-Rent War they fight cloaked as "Indians," and their actions lead to a law that displaces countless Indigenous Americans. Settlers are sent out to establish single farms in hundreds of acres that add up to hundreds of thousands of acres across the country, all of it Indigenous territory. Those settlers are citizen colonizers establishing single farms. The Homestead Act spreads private ownership as small-scale capitalism across the country.

On the cusp of the Civil War, the Anti-Rent uprising flares again, and this time Calico Indians and Indigenous people are linked. It is 1859, and a group of Mohicans, members of the Stockbridge-Munsee nation, return to their traditional lands, on what the tribe calls "national business." They work with Anti-Renters to identify and occupy vacant farms. Mohican is an Anglicization of their name, Muh-he-conneok. They are the people from the place where the waters perpetually flow, for the Hudson River that is their homeland. Across the Hudson from me, the Livingston family claimed hundreds of thousands of contested acres as part of their land patent. The territory is never sold or ceded. There is no treaty or agreement.

It is and was plain theft. It still is Mohican land (and here is the place where past and present are continuous with our moment). The same is true in much of Delaware County where the Hardenbergh Patent surveyors lie to the Munsee Lenape inhabitants—and I suspect Oneidas too—as the officials map and measure the territory. These deceptions are key to the Anti-Renters' claims in the 1840s. If the titles are based on subterfuge, landlords don't own the land. Fourteen years after the shoot-out at Moses Earle's, Anti-Renters and Mohicans come together to challenge the title. The state supreme court refuses take up the case. The Stockbridge-Munsee men are heroes in two nations: first in their own for trying to recover the land, and then in the United States, where they serve on the Union side in the Civil War. They enlist, serve, fight, and die.

The Mohicans and Munsee have banded together since the eighteenth century as a way to survive European colonization. First they live in Stockbridge, MA, and then are driven west to Oneida territory, near where my parents lived. As the Oneidas are also forced off their land, the Munsees and Mohicans move to Indiana (to what is called now Muncie, Indiana) and finally Wisconsin where they still live as a combined nation, the Stockbridge-Munsee, together.

Despite the dispersals, disease, disenfranchisement, and death—all the ways to separate people from their lands and culture—these nations are resilient. The word *Lenape* means people, the original people, the real people. What is profound is a homecoming happening now, where the people, the Munsee and Mohicans and others, are returning. Some have never left. Some intermarried and hid their traditions and cultures to preserve them. Or, there's Bonney Hartley, a Stockbridge-Munsee historian who lives in the upper Hudson Valley. She works to protect crucial historical and cultural sites, and ensures that the tribe has a national presence here, that these connections endure, and that her community in Wisconsin and those upstate are linked. Last year the 156 acres of Papscanee Island, named for the Mohican sachem who lived there, whose land was "sold" to the first Van Rensselaer patroon, was returned to Stockbridge-Munsee ownership.

—

Walking across the top of Hubbell Hill, David points out the NO TRESPASSING signs. We also have them nailed into trees at the property line. They're supposed to be for liability: someone gets injured and they can't sue because they're trespassing. The notices guard every farm and house along the road, along the land that people here dreamed could be public, could be a commons.

Some of the signs are orange, others yellow or white. They come in metal and Tyvek. Ours are die-cut plastic. I stop to read a metal one nailed into a tree. The bark grows into the edge of the steel. POSTED PRIVATE LANDS. The words are in two typefaces, one with serifs as if to underline the private part.

—

The anti-mask law was still being used in 2011 to prosecute Occupy Wall Street and is only rescinded when the pandemic begins, because we all need to wear masks.

—

I leave NYU to teach at a school where they promise that they have the highest number of Pell Grants per capita. Still, there is debt. I think of my neighbors and my students, teaching and peonage, the debt that forces them into capitalism. One of the justifications for tenancy was against laziness. Just making enough to get by wasn't okay. People needed to be dragged into capitalism and its cruelties. My students are forced into capitalism by debt. It drives them to get credentials, to get a job, to get a certain standard of living to pay off the debt—and there's how my neighbors fought all peonage. Over the last decade college debt has doubled since the housing crisis. It's nearly a trillion dollars—more than all the medical debt and credit card debt in the country combined. It also implicitly perpetuates racial and gender inequities. A white family gets a return of $55,869 on an investment in a college degree, a Black family doesn't even get a tenth of that, not even five thousand dollars, and a Latinx one even less. There is an uprising waiting to happen.

—

Now in this present of writing it is Thanksgiving and Christmas and New Year's:

Thanksgiving Day: a car accident, a snowy rural road, a car in the ditch. Christmas Day: a flood and New Year's Day: a medevac helicopter, a landing zone set up by the river in our village park. For the flood I wake at 3:30 in the morning. Several inches of rain fall on several feet of snow.

As I write this that Christmas morning I am in a Subaru on a state highway; soggy, wet, and hungry. An hour later dawn breaks, and men in hunting boots and blaze-orange camo wait with another man in a florescent VFD vest emblazoned with reflective silver tape. The three of them stand together in the road, shift their weight, and watch the waters.

> Florescent: Socialism, Venezuela, it used to be fine.
> Another: In Canada you get something serious, then you die. You have to wait on the line.
> The third: None of that socialism here.

I sidle to my car to write it down as the mud-red water reaches the intersection. I want to say the best health care I ever had was in London. I want to tell them about the uprising.

On New Year's, waiting for the helicopter:

"Socialists—" one says.

"Venezuela . . . used to be—" It's that line again from a different person now.

"If they come for my stuff," the first says, "I've got my backhoe . . ."

"That election, you wonder why three times as many people voted as there are citizens."

"You gotta look in the graveyards."

"—and illegals."

Cue my frozen miserable smile. The conversation continues. Someone asks if I am cold. I cannot say I am angry. I do not say anything. I wonder if my showing up says enough?

"My mother talked about Lithuania—"

To which I do not mention pogroms or my own family's flight, escaping shtetels and ghettos. Or how beyond my immediate family, they are all dead. I assume this person is talking of communism, that was the problem in Lithuania.

"History repeats itself," they say.

But I do not say that it does, or anything about the cross burned on my dad's lawn when he was eight—or any of the other events that look to me like repetitions. I am still an outsider and still scared to draw attention to myself.

—

In the present time I stare out at snowy fields on land where John Clum collected rocks. The piles are dazzling and beautiful. I feel lucky to see them. Ice crystals catch the light, tossing up prisms of red and blue, a rainbow scintillating in the snow. Human time lends itself to thinking there's an order to time, or maybe just white colonizers see this order, inscribed with the narratives of history and conquering, with once seeing the land as empty. I'm writing this in what feels like interstitial time, the gaps of time, and to write this is a kind of marginalia. One of the last index cards to go on my wall comes from the *New York Times*: "Yet Another Covid Victim: Capitalism." I hope so. These words and ideas are messy and maybe that is a victory.

It is January and deep drifts line the roads. We hike across the fields of Muriel and her father and Augustus. Gray tips of goldenrod pierce the snow. It is so deep it buoys us up nearly a foot higher in the air. We reach the mill and falls that she and Augustus never owned. They are a relic, "a relict." The word means a delinquent piece of land. It is leftover, unclaimed, a wasteland, some would say. I have found the carcass of a deer here, and old beer cans, but this waterfall once represented power and capitalism. On one tree the posted sign is half torn off. Around us new snow muffles all sounds. There are no cars, and even our breath seems stilled. I grab at the sign, and David laughs. The Tyvek flutters to the ground.

What are you doing? What if someone drives up?

Like who? The roads are closed. I'm making it free. For all, for all of us. I say. I don't mention Brisbane but he's here, so is my father, and so are you.

I rip down another sign and it floats into the waterfall.

Notes

The epigraph comes from Benjamin's "Theses on the Philosophy of History" (also called "On the Concept of History"). I too can't say "this is how it really was," but rather, this is how it seems to me in this time, another moment of danger.

Benjamin's essay on history was his last work, written in 1940, just months before he killed himself on the French/Spanish border. He was talking about history at a terrifying time. The essay comes in numbered fragments, as if fragments were all that was left—or all that was possible—in that crisis. Order and narrative were unmanageable or intolerable, because the urgency of the moment required a different sort of writing.

The next fragment, no. 7, is about empathy, about living in the past. Benjamin writes here about "the historians who wish to relive an era." They should, he says, "blot out what they know of the course of history." This is "a process of empathy." I might be that writer, even as I am no historian. I want to recreate the spirit of the Anti-Rent War, which can be seen as a bead on a thread of similar uprisings whose urgency and lessons are rarely considered and rarely linked.

Living here in these old, scrubbed-down mountains, I have come to experience history as alive and held in a place. For me time is dimensional and all at once, a kind of polytemporality. But, I am also here in the writing and the research for "the spark of hope," something Benjamin mentions too. And, I am here with the dead, with the gravestones and other stones that line the roads and fields where I live. For me the past feels alive, and Benjamin's form, the fragment, feels as apt for our time as his.

The Benjamin quote above is from *Illuminations*, ed. Hannah Arendt, trans. Harry Zohn (New York: Schocken Books, 1988), pp. 253–264. The epigraph comes from a slightly different translation in the Walter Benjamin Archive on marxists.org. "On the Concept of History," trans. Dennis Redmond. https://www.marxists.org/reference /archive/benjamin/1940/history.htm.

In my work, the opening chapter with the shoot-out in the corral is a synthesis of many sources, histories, lithographs, and contemporary newspaper accounts, as well as records of the weather and my own knowledge of plants and weeds and farming in the Western Catskills. The bulk of the research, though, comes from testimony taken just after the shooting. A panel of three state judges, akin to a grand jury, sat in Delhi every day but Sunday. They met morning into night for a month from the day after the shooting, August eighth, until September eleventh. The testimony they recorded is all handwritten. Sometimes the notes trail off; other times, reading them, you can see the judges' and court reporter's Anti-Rent biases. They are barely concealed. The testimony was typed up by Shirley Houck, who worked in the county clerk's office until her death in 2013 and was the Delhi Village Historian. Without her work, it would have been impossible for me to untangle all the fountain pen flourishes from 1845.

The testimony, which anyone can read in the Delhi County Courthouse, records the proceedings of August seventh, 1845, from multiple perspectives and also relates the events of months earlier that led up to that day. Hundreds were arrested and dragged before the panel, including many who were not at the shooting. Reading the testimony over and over again, it becomes clear what happened at Moses Earle's farm, who said what, and who did what. What remains unknown is who shot Steele. Much of the dialogue I included comes directly from that testimony, except for small instances where I imagine, say, Wright asking Sheriff Moore where the two other lawmen were, and where was the posse they promised to bring. I love the language in the testimony. Written without much punctuation, it's dated and jarring and beautiful. The corral fences are "bars," and instead of riding side-by-side as they leap the fence, Steele and the constable Edgerton come "side a side" in the documents.

The histories I use throughout the book are listed at the back. John D. Monroe, my county's historian in the 1940s, wrote about the Anti-Rent War just before he died, and my neighbor Steve Miller swears his is the best account—because his father swore it was the best account. His father staged the hundredth anniversary reenactment, and I take Ivan Miller via Steve Miller's endorsement seriously.

Reading Monroe's introduction, his rage on behalf of the tenant farmers is palpable. This anger runs through almost all of the accounts, including Henry Christman's history written on the hundredth anniversary in 1945 and Dorothy Kubik's more recently. Christman and Kubik both include indexes of Anti-Rent songs. In the first chapter I use one of Christman's that goes to the tune of "Oh Dear What Can the Matter Be." In his version, the Anti-Renters had already changed the lyrics, as happens often with folk songs. I changed them more, making them Andes specific, imagining what they'd have sung that morning.

Mayham and Christman spell Sheriff Greene Moore's name as More. Sometimes in the testimony it's spelled that way, but in ads in the Delaware Gazette in 1845, he's spelled as Moore, so I am using that spelling.

I'm especially grateful to contemporary historians Reeve Huston and Mark Lause. (Also the only two historians I consult with no connection to the Catskills.) They have examined the larger forces around the Anti-Rent War, especially ties to radical reform ideals and utopian socialism and worker's movements. These ideals are reflected in the testimony and are drawn out in Christman's history.

A lithograph in the Library of Congress, *The Death of Osman N. Steele*, helped me picture the scene at Earle's farm. From this I deduced what the lawyer Wright was wearing. The fashion of the era for men of aspiration included nipped waists that required a corset. The laborers and tenants would have worn much rougher clothes, including a long shirt that would they wrap around them in the place of drawers.

While the exact date of the image is unknown, a handwritten note at the bottom of the Library of Congress print says it was "deposited in the clerks office for the Southern District of New York Sept 20, 1845," so must have been made soon after the shooting. You can find it on the Library of Congress website under the Prints and Photographs Division at https://www.loc.gov/item/2003665079/ and a color version as a part of the Harry T. Peters "America on Stone" Lithography Collection on the Smithsonian Institution's National Museum of American History website, https://americanhistory.si.edu/collections/search /object/nmah_324900.

Finally, most of the Calico Indians' disguises were burned and otherwise destroyed after the shooting. I couldn't have written any of this without access to Rudd Hubbell's mask. The mask with the Poseidon badge on it is held in the collection of the Andes Society for History and Culture at the Hunting Tavern, where Osman Steele had his last drink on the morning of August 7, 1845.

Chapter 2

26   *Right now, in the bit I'm hanging* Elizabeth Hardwick, "Writing a Novel," *New York Review of Books*, October 18, 1973, accessed October 17, 2017, https://www.nybooks .com/articles/1973/10/18/writing-a-novel/?prin.

28   *Pakatakan is Munsee Lenape land* Hekan is supposed to be a traditional Munsee name, and I find his name listed as Kakawaremin and other spellings. In documents that refer to him, his name changes first to the Dutch in 1707 and by 1719 is only listed as his Dutch name. "Appendix, Natives' Profiles," in *Munsee Indian Trade in Ulster County, New York, 1712-1732*, eds. Kees-Jan Waterman, J. Michael Smith; trans. Kees-Jan Waterman (Syracuse: Syracuse University Press, 2013), pp. 256–261. Stable URL: https://www.jstor.org/stable/j.ctt1j2n99p.12.

30   *Over the time I live here* From a May 30, 2023, email with Diane Galusha, Middletown Town Historian and author of *Liquid Assets: A History of New York City's Water*

System. And a June 3, 2023, email with Shelly J. Johnson-Bennett; Director of the Delaware County Department of Planning and Watershed Affairs. Both of them stress that the numbers are always in flux, always increasing for the city because it is constantly acquiring more land.

Chapter 4

40   *Another of Rich's poems* The two books are Adrienne Rich, *Blood, Bread, and Poetry: Selected Prose, 1979–1985* (New York: Norton, 1986), and *A Wild Patience Has Taken Me This Far: Poems 1978–1981* (New York: Norton 1981).

      "What Is Possible," pp. 23–25.

      The cascading lines about "class privilege" are from "Heroines," p. 33.

41   *I joked that our outer suburb* In London, I lived on the edge of Brixton and Herne Hill. The latter was Ruskin's neighborhood. The Clash's "The Guns of Brixton," released in 1979, predates the 1981 Brixton riots that happened on the street where I would come to live.

42   *Here is Rich too, "marking" Addams's life* From "Culture and Anarchy," *A Wild Patience*, p. 12.

      Adrienne Rich's writing of history as inhabitation set out a model for what history could be. For her it's a version of feminist history as a corrective, like Linda Nochlin's *Why Have There Been No Great Women Artists*. This way of writing the past—not as a history itself but as inhabitation—has slept inside me for years. It's a bit Ruskin-like too, in that he imagined into history alternatives to the capitalism of his present, using Gothic architecture, which is just plain ridiculous, but beautiful too . . .

      I love too, both now and then, when I was a teen, how Rich used the material conditions of women's lives to ask about us, our ambitions and possibilities.

45   *Five little cows and a tiny couple*   Asher Brown Durand, *High Point: Shandaken Mountains*, 1853, oil on canvas, 32 ¾ x 48" (83.2 x 121.9 cm), Metropolitan Museum of Art, New York.

48   *Reds Battle Police*   "Reds Battle Police in Rent Strike Riot," *New York Times*, January 23, 1932.

        2802 Olinville Avenue, "the communist quarter in the Bronx," on Google Street View, currently (in 2023) shows people huddled in the cold in February of 2022, and another man in a blue anorak and camo pants. All of their faces are blurred. Signs on the building declare: DO NOT LOITER, and <u>POSITIVELY</u> NO BALL PLAYING ALLOWED.

49   *We need the women*   From "1,500 Fight Police to Aid Rent Strike: 100 Men Break through Lines and Chase Aged Landlord through Bronx Streets. Woman Bites Chauffeur but No Arrests Are Made as Aides of Marshal Evict Twenty Families from Five Houses," *New York Times*, February 27, 1932. Also, they blow a ram's horn to rouse the protesters. In the Anti-Rent War a tin horn is used that had been used to call in workers for lunch from the fields.

49   *During World War I, women in Glasgow*   While the men are off fighting in World War I (a war that impacted working-class Britons particularly) the women fight the landlords. See William Gallacher, *Revolt on the Clyde: An Autobiography*, 2nd ed. (1936; repr., London: Lawrence and Wishart, 1978).

        And: Alan Dawson, "Red Clydeside: A Digital History of the Labour Movement in Glasgow 1910–1932," Glasgow Digital Library website, accessed December 12, 2022, http://gdl.cdlr.strath.ac.uk/redclyde/.

50   *Or, Pauline Newman*   See Glyn Robbins, "New York's Winter Rent Strike Inspired Generations," *Jacobin Magazine*, December 12, 2021, https://jacobin.com/2021/12/nyc -1907-rent-strike-paulina-newman-east-side-housing. See

also Tony Michels, "Uprising of 20,000 (1909)" *Shalvi/
Hyman Encylcopedia of Jewish Women* (December 31,
1999), Jewish Women's Archive (website), https://jwa.org
/encyclopedia/article/uprising-of-20000-1909.

50   *The people are mightier*   James Hunter, "The Politics
of Highland Land Reform, 1873–1895" *The Scottish
Historical Review* 53, no. 155, part 1 (April 1974): pp. 45–
68. (Also: The Highland Land League was modeled on the
Irish Land League which eventually became the IRA.)

51   *The uprising begins as a country doctor*   See Christman,
pp. 58 and 62–63.

51   *The Anti-Renters proclaim*   For more on this part of Anti-
Rent War history see John D. Monroe, Reeve Huston,
and Henry Christman, as well as Stewart Holbrook's
"Rebellions on the Manors,"chap. 3 of Part IV, in *Dreamers
of the American Dream* (New York: Doubleday, 1957), pp.
134–145.

Chapter 5

55   *This rambling is transcendent*   Henry David Thoreau,
"Walking," *The Atlantic* (June 1862), https://www
.theatlantic.com/magazine/archive/1862/06/walking
/304674/.

55   *I think too of Harriet Martineau*   Michael R. Hill, "An
Introduction to Harriet Martineau's Lake District
Writings," in *An Independent Woman's Lake District
Writings* by Harriet Martineau, ed. Michael R. Hill
(Amherst, NY: Humanity Books, 2004), pp. 25–54.

Harriet Martineau, "Under a Spell," from "1844
Tynemouth," republished from her book *Letters on
Mesmerism*, in *Lapham's Quarterly* online, accessed
December 12, 2022, https://www.laphamsquarterly.
org/magic-shows/under-spell.

"Serious Work: Harriet Martineau," Women in the Hills (website), accessed February 28, 2022, https://womeninthehills.co.uk/2020/03/23/serious-work-harriet-martineau/.

57 *John Burroughs, a nature writer from the Catskills* "The Exhilarations of the Road," in "Winter Sunshine," from *The Writings of John Burroughs*, vol. 2 (1875; Project Gutenberg, July 2003), https://www.gutenberg.org/files/4279/4279-h/4279-h.htm#link2I I_4_0004.

63 *So too is getting this call* It's a sign of American capitalism that these white people, my parents, who grew up poor and valued co-ops, got a mortgage (not even one because of my dad's serving in World War II) and bought a home, then sold it after I was born and got another home, a bigger home. In this, wealth accumulated. Even living in a Virginia suburb that had no racist covenants, no redlining, that had Black residents, this was the case. Yet, these mortgages with their mortgage-interest tax breaks are block grants for whiteness. Here at the end of their lives, my parents have a financial planner, and that planner calls me and offers a HELOC. It boggles my mind the speed at which wealth has been built upon property ownership for white people in the United States.

Chapter 6

67 *I'm teaching a class on place* In the middle of the pandemic, in the final year of School of Visual Art's Art Writing MFA program, I taught a short seminar on place, on Zoom. I'm grateful to the students, my colleagues and comrades in this, who were up to try this experiment—as we were all cut off from each other and disembodied—to explore place together. That class included Jenny Monick, Kate Brock, Nyasha Chiundiza, Geronimo Cristobal, Enos Nyamor

Otieno, and Seoung Eun Bae. This Moment Part III:
Place, SVA Art Writing MFA, Fall 2020. Jenny Monick
brought in the Whitman poem "To a Stranger," published in
Leaves of Grass in 1867, and the Carter Family song "Hello
Stranger" (released as the B side of "Never Let the Devil Get
the Upper Hand of You" in 1937). And she brought the idea
that place is the moment, the possibility between two people.

Chapter 7

75 *he laughs and tells us* The grouse is amazing to watch
drum. The bird is wasteful, dynamic, beautiful, ridiculous
and there are links to watch videos of male ruffled grouse
drumming on Youtube. See for example https://www
.youtube.com/watch?v=tcA3tyE1fYs or https://www
.youtube.com/watch?v=q0obByQW23k.

76 *He follows HELPP* The acronym HELPP comes from
Soren Eriksson's Game of Logging, a safety training
program for forestry for both professional loggers and
amateurs; that is, landowners who need to fell trees for
reasons from firewood to forest health.

77 *All of Margaretville, all of my town* For more on the
Hardenbergh Patent see: Alf Evers, *The Catskills: From
Wilderness to Woodstock*, rev. ed. (New York: Abrams
Books, 1982), pp. 33–64.

    John D. Monroe, *Chapters in the History of Delaware
County New York*, pp. 13–23.

78 *George Washington meanwhile* In fact Washington does
win one of the Hardenbergh Patent parcels, but is never
given the prize. Evers, p. 127.

78 *These accusations of laziness appear* The concept of
laziness as a sin seems foundational for the United
States. In the Massachusetts Bay Colony, the elect—
those who were close to God—were the most successful.

In the South this notion of laziness too was used to justify enslaving others.

81   *The 1837 recession* See Chris Jennings, *Paradise Now: The Story of American Utopianism* (New York: Random House, 2016), pp. 177–178. His awesome history is largely devoted to the utopian experiments in the wake of the crisis.

Samuel Rezneck, "The Social History of an American Depression, 1837–1843," *The American Historical Review* 40, no. 4 (July 1935): pp. 662–687. See also Stephen Campbell, "Panic of 1837," *The Economic Historian* (website), August 15, 2022, accessed December 12, 2022, https://economic-historian.com/2020/11/panic-of-1837/.

81   *the* Huge Paw, Log Cabin, Whig Star Christman, pp. 54, 55.

Chapter 8

87   *In the sunroom now, I study* The new barn is mentioned in the column "Mountain Dew," *Catskill Mountain News,* July 26, 1946.

"Neighbors Make Hay for Farmer Hurt Saturday: Ralph Scott Caught by Rope Cannot Work for a Long Time," *Catskill Mountain News,* July 15, 1949, and July 29, 1949.

"Took Vows Saturday, Mr. and Mrs. Henry Robinson," *Catskill Mountain News,* August 20, 1964.

90   *I stare at their wedding announcement* "In 1940 a daughter was born—" from: "Local and Personal" *Catskill Mountain News,* August 16, 1940.

"Delaware County Fair Huge Success Closed Friday Night: Local Boys Win in Potato and Poultry Judging Contests. Plane Crashes. Ralph Scott Takes Prize for Best Ayrshire Cow," *Catskill Mountain News,* August 29, 1947.

91   *The local feed store runs an ad* "Our Roster of Fine Dairies," Dugan & Taber ad, *Catskill Mountain News,* February 23, 1951.

Chapter 9

95   *I learn that Moses Earle subscribes* For more, see Evers, p. 415.

96   *If it had happened after the Civil War* Mayham, p. 84.

96   *One historian, Reeve Huston* Huston, *Land and Freedom*, pp. 116–119.

97   *Another account by Harvard historian* Philip J. Deloria, *Playing Indian* (New Haven: Yale University Press), 1998, chapters 1–2, specifically pp. 23–25, 28, 40.

97   *In a search of the car* Lissa Harris, "K-9 Osman 'Ozzie' Steele Makes His First Arrest," *The Watershed Post*, September 13, 2013, posted 3:57 p.m., http://www.watershedpost.com/2013/k-9-osman-ozzie-steele-makes-his-first-arrest, accessed 4/6/22.

99   *and this school, one of the wealthiest* For more on NYU's holdings and wealth, see: Aleksey Bilogur, "Who Are the Biggest Landowners in New York City," analyzing public data on his blog *Aleksey Bilogur*, May 27, 2016, https://www.residentmar.io/2016/05/27/biggest-landowners-nyc.html. And Matthew Schuerman, "NYU, Columbia Make a Mint on Real Estate," *The Observer* (website), May 1, 2006, https://observer.com/2006/05/nyu-columbia-make-a-mint-on-real-estate/; as well as Tanay Warerkar, "New York's 10 Biggest Property Owners," *Curbed New York* (website), September 14, 2018, https://ny.curbed.com/2018/9/14/17860172/new-york-10-biggest-property-owners, all accessed 5/13/2022.

100   *that wave in my mom's hair* I steal that image of Veronica Lake and her hair from Ted Hughes describing the first moment he saw Sylvia Plath. Ted Hughes, "Fulbright Scholars," *Birthday Letters* (London: Faber and Faber, 1998), p. 3.

100   *She is an economist* I grew up in Hollin Hills, a mid-century modernist subdivision outside Washington, DC,

that was a left-wing utopia. Until it wasn't. For more, see my essay "The Fairytale," in *Granta* (online edition), December 1, 2016, https://granta.com/the-fairytale/.

104   *I read another writer, Yiyun Li, talk* Yiyun Li interviewed by Eve Bowman for the *New York Review of Books* Newsletter (email), March 5, 2022.

105   *This was also a significant moment* "Mystery of Fossilized Trees Is Solved," *ScienceDaily*, April 19, 2007, https://www.sciencedaily.com/releases/2007/04/070418130435.htm.

Chapter 10

109   *Two Christian pastors make the news* Adam Gabbatt, "'Blood Moon' Brings Prophecies of End Times—but Nasa Says Not to Worry," *The Guardian*, September 27, 2015, https://www.theguardian.com/world/2015/sep/27/blood-moon-apocalypse-nasa-lunar-eclipse-supermoon.

Chapter 11

118   *Anger helps people feel in control* Anger creates a sense of control, and there are links between pain and anger; meanwhile we are in an opioid crisis, and this crisis is fueled by capitalism, by a need for profits, and many of those in pain who are medicating themselves against it (and against the pain capitalism has caused them) are also enraged. Or, put another way, their justified rage is getting smothered in pain meds, while chronic pain causes frustration and anger. All of this makes me think of capitalism and how with the neoliberal policies that shape contemporary America many people earn less, face more instability, and have no recourse to fix this, so pain. Or pain drugs.

Bernard Golden, "What Is the Link Between Anger and Physical Pain?" *Psychology Today* (website), July 16, 2021, https://www.psychologytoday.com/gb/blog/overcoming -destructive-anger/202107what-is-the-link-between -anger-and-physical-pain.

And Rosemary Black, "When Chronic Pain Leads to Chronic Anger," HealthCentral (website), May 11, 2020, https://www.healthcentral.com/pain-management /chronic-pain-anger-strategies.

119   *Called a Beers map for its publisher*   A copy is available on the Delaware County NY Genealogy Website, https://www .dcnyhistory.org/BeersAtlas1869/MiddletownLowRes .jpg.

121   *I sell the shadow to support the substance*   This is the legend that runs on a series of carte de visite Sojourner Truth posed for and sold to support her work with abolition and supporting Black war veterans and hospitals in the Civil War.

Chapter 12

126   *Why aren't we organizing them?*   "IWW Interview with Noam Chomsky: Worker Occupations and the Future of Radical Labor," IWW Website, October 9, 2009, accessed May 30, 2021, https://archive.iww.org/history /library/Chomsky/2009int/.

128   *The said Louisa M*   All of the deeds are held in the Delaware County Courthouse, Delhi, NY. This specific deed is Liber 56, pp. 90–91, dated December 8, 1862, and recorded January 17, 1863 at 8 a.m. by R.S. Hughston, clerk.

130   *I find a Peter Clumb in my township*   In an age before standardized spellings the name went from Klum, to Clum but also included Clumb, similar to how Kittle was also spelled Kettle.

132   *Here lies Philip Klum*   From Find a Grave (website), accessed December 12, 2022, https://www.findagrave.com/memorial/107797781/philip-klum. (Roger Davis, who has worked at our transfer station, posted the image. He is an amazing local historian.)

Chapter 13

137   *David and I watch that movie*   The movie is *Northern Lights*, 1978, produced, written and directed by John Hanson and Rob Nilsson. Shot in 16mm, it is filmed on location in North Dakota—in winter—using farmers as extras and won a Caméra d'Or at Cannes.

Chapter 14

145   *The land is mine saith the Lord*   From Mayham, p. 40. "2 cents an acre, to support the uprising. Those without land pay 2 pounds," from Monroe, *The Anti Rent War*, p. 118; Kubik, p. 48.; and Christman, p. 84. "Awake, Arouse" and the Fourth of July organizing, Chrisman, pp. 79–80 and 84–85. "Last appeals fail," Christman, p. 86.

145   *It is a Tuesday, September third*   Monroe, *Anti-Rent War*, pp. 18–19; and *New-York Tribune*, September 4, 1844.

145   *to choose a slate of candidates*   Huston, p. 104.

151   *will take up arms*   David's right to happiness wasn't about joy, not originally. It is tied to wealth, to an "estate," to property. One of the origins of "happiness" in Jefferson's "self-evident truths" in the Declaration of Independence is Locke's statement that society exists "to protect life, liberty and estate"—so the state exists to protect property and capitalism. But also that happiness equals property.

151 *They had either got to fight or die* Kubik, p. 27.

151 *They spoil distress sales on February first* Kubik, pp. 42–43.

151 *One historian calls him* Christman, p. 134; "Bold, forward and officious," is from Monroe, *Anti-Rent War*, p. 17, quoting *History of Delaware County, NY* (New York: W.W. Munsell, 1880), p. 68.

151 *A couple of years before the war* Monroe, *The Anti-Rent War*, p. 19.

151 *Our Country Has Been in Great Commotion* Delaware Gazette, March 19, 1845.

152 *The lawmen abduct Zera Preston* Kubik, p. 57.

152 *In the bar he jokes* Monroe, *The Anti-Rent War*, p. 20.

152 *The legend: Free soil. Free people* The word "free" meant not enslaved—free trade, free labor, all of these "freedoms" were against the slavery system of the South, and the Republican party's clarion cry of free trade hearkens back to that, even as it means trade with no boundaries or restrictions today.

152 *A WPA artist painted the mural there* The mural is *Down-Rent War, Around 1845* by Mary Earley, 1940, winner of the 1939 "48-State Competition" for post office murals. For more information see: http://wpamurals .org/48states.htm.

155 *These deeds reveal a world* See Zachary Veith, "Enslaved and in Service 1: Colonial New York," Staatsburgh State Historic Site (blog), May 5, 2022, http://staatsburgh statehistoricsite.blogspot.com/2022/05/enslaved-in -service-i-colonial-new-york.html#more.

155 *This "distrain and distress"* Distrain, according to *Merriam-Webster*, means "to force or compel to satisfy an obligation by means of a distress." Accessed May 30, 2023, https://www.merriam-webster.com/dictionary/distrain. And this "distress" is the sale of those seized goods, though it can also mean seizing those goods.

156 *'Today' is an impossible word for me* Ingeborg Bachmann, *Malina*, trans. Philip Boehm (New York: New Directions, 2019), p. 4.

157 *I think of Marx and his dancing tables* Karl Marx, "The Fetishism of the Commodity and Its Secret," chap. 1, part 4 in *Capital: A Critique of Political Economy*, trans. Ben Fowkes, vol. 1 (New York: Penguin, 1976; repr. 1982), p. 163.

Chapter 15

162 *Everyone "has a draft community* Jennings, *Paradise Now*, p. 190.

163 *and the word "individualism"* See usage of the word's developing in the *OED* but also in Harry Ritter's discussion of socialism in *Dictionary of Concepts in History* (Westport, CT: Greenwood Press, 1986).

163 *They have had to flee Germany* The Amanas later become famous in the twentieth century for manufacturing stoves and refrigerators. The Oneidas turn to producing flatware after their community fails.

164 *They open a grocery store* And, this grocery store is on Toad Lane, just outside Manchester. Nearly a century earlier, Ann Lee, founder of the Shakers, is also born on Toad Lane according to Chris Jennings's *Paradise Now*. In my dream world of overlapping socialisms, these facts are not separate, and this tiny street is a kind of ground zero for socialist possibility.

165 *and in the United States Greeley* He first publishes *Self Help by the People* in the United States in 1857. My copy is a later, expanded edition: George Jacob Holyoake, *Self Help by the People: The History of the Rochdale Pioneers, 1844–1892*, tenth ed. (New York: Charles Scribner's and Sons, 1900). I love the epigraph "from nothing . . . grew

everything." Holyoake is also listed on the title page as "author of *The History of Co-operation in England* and *Sixty Years of an Agitator's Life* etc., etc."

167 *The poet Ian Parks writes of goldenrod* Ian Parks, "Goldenrod," *Shell Island* (Oxfordshire: Waywiser Press, 2006), p. 11.

Parks, who's from Yorkshire, studies and writes on Chartist poetry. The final poem in his collection *Citizens* (Ripon, UK: Smokestack Books, 2017) is "Elegy for the Chartist Poets." Parks's PhD dissertation draws on the Chartist newspaper the *Northern Star* (where Devyr also was published and sent regular letters back to the UK from the Anti-Rent uprising). For more see "Ian Parks and His Version of the North," in Strange Alliances (blog), April 2, 2013, accessed December 14, 2022, https://strangealliances.wordpress.com/2013/04/02/ian-parks-and-his-version-of-the-north/.

Chapter 16

170 *Gould is writing* Jay Gould, *History of Delaware County and Border Wars of New York Containing a Sketch of the Early Settlements in the County and a History the Late Anti-Rent Difficulties in Delaware with other Historical and Miscellaneous Matter Never Before Published* (Roxbury: Keeny & Gould Publishers, 1856). Specifically on the Anti-Rent War see section 7; for Anti-Rent troubles, chapters 9–13.

172 *Mr. Jay Gould Assaulted* New York Times, August 3, 1877.

173 *The theme of the articles read* From "The Anarchists' Trial: Bullets Put into Evidence by the Prosecution," the *New York Times*, July 27, 1886.

This is the Haymarket Trial, after strikes on May 1, 1886, supporting the eight-hour workday turn violent.

The strike lasts three days in Chicago. The police shoot into the crowd. The crowd meets the next day in Haymarket Square, and just as the protests are breaking up, the police charge, and someone throws a bomb. No one knows who—cop, protester, Pinkerton? Newspapers blame protesters. The left is divided and turns anti-immigrant. Anyone who is German is a suspect. Anarchists are rounded up. In the resulting trial, the judge—Judge Gary, in whose court the woman in the white lawn dress appears—refuses to seat any union members on the jury and taunts the defendants. All eight are found guilty. Four are hanged. One commits suicide. The men are martyrs. May first is for most of the world May Day, Labor Day, International Workers' Day . . . Everywhere but the United States. And that seems political, a way of shying away from both the mass labor movement that coalesced to protest in May and the violence at the heart of workers organizing. In the Haymarket incidents I see historical repetitions of protests and police retribution that play out over and over again, similar to the scene at Moses Earle's farm.

173   *Another article, another day*   Testimony that Gould should be hanged or thrown in the lake, as well as "the woman in the dress of white lawn," from "The Anarchists' Trial: New Witnesses Strengthen the Prosecution," *New York Times*, July 28, 1886.

173   *Now the three richest Americans*   Chuck Collins and Josh Hoxie, *Billionaire Bonanza 2017: The Forbes 400 and the Rest of Us*, a report published by the Institute for Policy Studies, November 8, 2017, p. 2.

174   *his family establishes a rec center*   On Twitter a writer who has written a biography of Gould tweets at me that Gould "made significant anonymous gifts" to NYU and "saved George Washington's Mt Vernon." Somehow that also seems fitting given the university's debt capitalism

and that Mount Vernon is home of the country's first president, with his land monopoly of hundreds of thousands of acres, not to mention his "owning" more than 300 people. The tweet quoted here is by Edward J. Renehan Jr. (@Ed_Renehan), September 23, 2022.

175 *I play Pete Seeger's version of the song* Pete Seeger, "Jay Gould's Daughter," *American Favorite Ballads, Vol. 5*, Smithsonian Folkways Recordings, 2007, https://youtu.be /fWQvtB4CMc0.

176 *The English 'liberal,' 'peace man,' 'philanthropist'* Searching for the term "world conventionist," eventually I find it in Google Books *The New Englander*, vol. 4, no. 8, January 1846, where on page 101, Jay Gould plagiarized an entire chapter about the Anti-Rent War—including those "World Conventionists." Which actually means the subtitle of his *History of Delaware County* that promises *"Other Historical and Miscellaneous Matter Never Before Published"* is, of course, a lie. My guess is that lying was not anathema to Gould, who swindled many, including his first business partner, Zadoc Pratt.

178 *he and his wife board a boat* Christman, p. 53.

178 *He talks of "oppression" as well* Christman, pp. 167 and 55–57.

178 *Vote Yourself a Farm* Lause, p. 63, and Christman, p. 71.

178 *In his 1847* Principles of Communism Evan Malmgren, "The Other American Frontier," *The Baffler*, April 18, 2022, accessed September 15, 2022, https://thebaffler .com/latest/the-other-american-frontier-malmgren.

179 *One of the organizers calls for change* Lause, p. 69.

179 *No man made the land* Testimony of Dr. Jonathan C. Allaben, August 1845.

179 *you now lived at Williamsburgh* Lumen Searle, Letter to the Editor, *The Albany Freeholder*, July 30, 1845. Transcribed for SUNY Oneonta by Terri Nan Ahrens in their collection "Voice of the People: Daily Life in the

Antebellum Rural Delaware County New York Area,"
accessed July 25, 2017.

179 *My neighbors pen odes and poems* These letters, songs,
and other documents were originally published online as
part of the digital collection "Daily Life in Antebellum
Rural New York: Reform/Conflict" by SUNY Oneonta,
accessed July 25, 2017.

Chapter 17

185 *The letter is addressed from* The leatherheads' letter is
in the collection of the Delaware County Historical
Association, Delhi, NY.

186 *There are ten thousand Calico Indians* Huston, p. 116.

187 *the Seneca are coerced* The initial treaty was a farce and
thrown out after many letters were written by Seneca
leaders and Quaker advocates to members of Congress,
and this second treaty—a compromise—was better, but
meant too that the Seneca were forced into a US version
of democracy, much less direct or democratic than their
nation's had been. Women lost power, only the men
could vote, and the consensus decision-making of the
Seneca's direct democracy was made unlawful. Some
Seneca opted to stay with traditional government but
lost their access to reservation lands. The United States
would not recognize or give tribal status to the group
that continued to follow traditional governance.

187 *they become adjuncts to a landscape* Wanda Nanibush,
Anishnawbe-kwe artist and curator, speaks eloquently
about this invisibility in landscape painting. Wanda
Nanibush interviewed by Sky Goodden, "A Rebuttal,
Not a Conversation: Discussing Ombaasin's AGO
Intervention, 'Land Rights Now'" *Momus*, June 23, 2015,
accessed March 10, 2021, http://momus.ca/a-rebuttal-not

-a-conversation-discussing-ombaasins-ago-intervention
-land-rights-now/.

188 *So, they lie and deceive to get the land* The quotes above are from Monroe, *Chapters in the History of Delaware County*, pp. 14–15. This deceit is part of what the Anti-Renters use as justification for their court cases against the landlords, challenging their title to the land.

188 *I think of Walt Whitman's "Calamus"* In the cycle "Calamus" from *Leaves of Grass* he writes too of "manly love, athletic love . . ." and "to celebrate the needs of my comrades." I know he means other men and love and sex, but what *I* want are comrades. (Also the poems in "Calamus" include "To A Stranger.") For more see *Leaves of Grass*, 1891–92, Walt Whitman Archive (online), "Calamus," https://whitmanarchive.org/published/LG /1891/poems/45.

190 *Devyr sees how property is power* Christman, pp. 152 and 156.

192 *invite everyone into their movement* Lause, p. 45.

193 *Steamboats and Rail Roads* The whole rollicking anarchist possibility of the NRA is in Lause, pp. 49, 51, 61.

193 *promise a "libertarian socialist future* Lause, p. 61.

194 *If force is used* Lause, p. 68.

194 *I read Devyr's obituary* Brooklyn Daily Eagle, May 28, 1887.

Chapter 19

205 *Devyr has suggested organizing bands* Christman, p. 74.

206 *As many as 200 indians* This quote and all those that follow in the chapter come from testimony given to the panel of three judges.

213 *After that fire Steele leaned himself forward* This text all comes from testimony given to the panel of three judges between August 8 and September 11, 1845.

The testimony is missing most punctuation, and while
I inserted periods, I kept the spelling, dashes, and
underlining of the original statements.

Chapter 20

222   *Their bayonets glittered*   Christman, p. 185.

222   *a tumble-down kind of a machine*   Christman, p. 185;
"Delhi Bastille" is what Dr. Jonathan Allaben called
the jail, Christman, p. 189; "strange legerdemain . . .
'American Robin Hood,'" p. 187.

223   *I never knew before I was somebody*   Christman, p. 187.
Brisbane wrote disparagingly about this photo to his
brother Robert (who'd been a Calico Indian), saying that
in it he "looked as grim and gray as old Tim Corbin in his
coat of tar and feathers." Corbin was one of the people
dispatched to send out notices for the landlords and the
first to be tarred and feathered in Roxbury (Monroe,
Anti-Rent War, p. 114).

224   *One lists Augustus Kittle*   From the court charges:
"Del. Gen. Sessions: The People vs Augustus Kittle &
12 others." "Indict Conspiracy, riot attempt to rescue
prisoners & appearing disguised & c", J. A. Hughston,
District Attorney, A true bill, John Edgerton foreman.
Filed Sept 12, 1845.

228   *Others, the green shields*   Joe Rankin, "Lichen
Not Technically a Plant," *Northern Woodlands*
(website), Outside Series, February 15, 2016, https://
northernwoodlands.org/outside_story/article/lichen
-not-technically-plant. Also see Joe Walewski *Lichens of
the North Woods: A Field Guide to 111 Northern Lichens*
(Duluth: Kollath+Stensaas, 2007).

231   *Devyr publishes in his paper*   Christman, p. 167.

232   *There is also Agatha Christie's* Endless Night   Agatha

Christie, *Endless Night* (London: Collins Crime Club, 1967); Harper Collins ebook edition, 2017.

233 *In prison, in the hastily constructed jail* Christman, pp. 187 and 193–195.

234 *Is it the Jankowsky's place?* I changed the name of the family to protect the privacy of the victims.

Chapter 21

238 *The poet Lisa Robertson writes* Lisa Robertson, *The Baudelaire Fractal* (Toronto: Coach House Books, 2020), p. 158.

239 *Lawrence Goodwyn is working on a book* Lawrence Goodwyn, *The Populist Moment: A Short History of the Agrarian Revolt in America* (London: Oxford University Press, 1978), pp. IX–XII.

His introduction talks about the failures of history and progress as clearly as Benjamin does in his *Theses*, where he takes aim at the very notion of progress. Goodwyn's footnotes too are an essay on history and its writing. He is an activist historian who examined how the Populist People's Party built a mass movement to oppose capitalism and how they taught, recruited, educated, and—in the post–Civil War era, in the South, at that—built cross-racial alliances. For him these aren't some distant lessons in the past, but strategies that we can use today still (even though his day was in the mid-1970s). For him the very idea of progress keeps the past dead, while for Benjamin the idea of progress and the present being preordained rationalized the Nazis' atrocities in his moment, so created death in this moment.

In one footnote on pp. 314–315, Goodwyn talks about the differences between American histories and novels (he prefers the latter, not surprisingly). Our histories, he says, "convey the national experience as a purposeful and generally progressive saga, almost divinely exonerated [. . .] from the vicissitudes elsewhere afflicting the human condition . . . [while] novelists [and I would add poets and essayists] [. . .] position themselves outside this narrow and uncreative orthodoxy."

Which takes me again to my comment at Steve Miller's: "this is maybe history or story, or just the narrative I need to tell . . ."

240 *Hardwick told one of her students* Darryl Pinckney, *Come Back in September: A Literary Education on West Sixty-Seventh Street, Manhattan* (New York: Farrar, Straus and Giroux, 2022), p. 6.

240 *and in this essay of hers on essays* Elizabeth Hardwick, "The Art of the Essay," in *The Uncollected Essays of Elizabeth Hardwick* (New York: New York Review Books, 2022), pp. 1–9.

241 *At his sentencing, one of them calls out* "The Anti-Rent Trials—Sentencing of the Prisoners—Lamentable Consequence of the Case," *Niles National Register*, October 18, 1845, p. 102.

241 *O! parents dear* Jailhouse letter of Edward O'Connor, October 1845, Collection of the Delaware County Historical Society. After he was freed from jail, he also wrote letters to and stayed with Muriel's forebearer, David Scott, and married Scott's daughter Jennet/Janet. He is writing to get help with his debts from the Anti-Rent War. Each Anti-Rent association had taken a collection to help those imprisoned.

241 *After he is free, Moses Earle* Monroe, *The Anti-Rent War*, pp. 106–107.

242 *the Anti-Rent uprising flares again* Warren F. Broderick, "Strange Partners in Land Equity: Mohicans and Tenant Farmers 'Invade' Upstate New York in 1859," *Hudson River Valley Review* 35, no. 2 (Spring 2019): pp. 13–25.

243   *They enlist, serve, fight, and die* The Stockbridge Munsee group includes Levi Kokapot, who went to Oberlin, served in the Civil War, died in that war. Others enlisted too: Joseph L. Chicks and John Chicks. He was older, sixty-three, and still he volunteered to fight. Another, Jesse Wybrow, went on to live near Ripon, Wisconsin at Fond du Lac, where Brisbane lived, as did other Anti-Rent organizers.

244   *was returned to Stockbridge-Munsee* The very idea of selling land, of owning land, of having title to land, was so foreign to the Lenape and the Mohicans that there wasn't even a word for it.

     "The Long Journey Home: The Return of New York's Papscanee Island to the Stockbridge-Munsee Community," A Story Map project by the Stockbridge-Munsee Community and the Open Space Institute, accessed on January 10, 2023, https://storymaps.arcgis.com/stories/4b5d61785b064ff49ceff158e05e89fb.

     For more on Bonney Hartley's work, see Josh Landes, "Stockbridge-Munsee Historic Preservation Manager Oversees Repatriation of Ancestral Artifacts from Berkshire Museum," for WAMC Northeast Public Radio, February 11, 2022, https://www.wamc.org/news/2022-02-11/stockbridge-munsee-historic-preservation-manager-oversees-repatriation-of-ancestral-artifacts-from-berkshire-museum. See also Clarence Fanto, "'We Have a Footprint on Main Street Again': 'Mohican Miles' Exhibit Opens in Stockbridge," *Berkshire Eagle*, July 5, 2021, https://www.berkshireeagle.com/news/southern_berkshires/we-have-a-footprint-on-main-street-again-mohican-miles-exhibit-opens-in-stockbridge/article_a615394c-ddc1-11eb-b904-87c47d2fb0c8.html.

245   *It's nearly a trillion dollars* PBS *Newshour*, May 20, 2022.

245   *A white family gets a return* See Laura Shin, "The Racial Wealth Gap: Why a Typical White Household Has 16 Times the Wealth of a Black One," *Forbes*, March 26,

2015, https://www.forbes.com/sites/laurashin/2015/
03/26/the-racial-wealth-gap-why-a-typical-white
-household-has-16-times-the-wealth-of-a-black-one.

247   *One of the last index cards* Farah Nayeri, "Yet Another
Covid Victim: Capitalism," *New York Times*, October 7,
2021. https://www.nytimes.com/2021/10/07/world
/covid-pandemic-capitalism-stiglitz-berville.html.

Images

15   Detail from *The Death of Osman N. Steele*, 1845. Based
on descriptions by Sheriff Greene Moore, Constable
Edgerton (the Undersheriff), and Lawyer Peter Wright,
the caption reads: "We the undersigned being present
at the scene of the murder of Undersheriff Steele do
Certify the above sketch to be a faithful representation
of the scene & accurate in every important particular."
From the collection of the Library of Congress.

16   In Andes, New York, a mile from the site of the shootout
at Moses Earle's, this is the only sign of what happened.

29   The fairy-tale home is on the far right. Undated postcard
addressed to Miss Josie Murphy, Rochester, New York,
mailed August 3, 1908.

38   Bob and Sandy Kabat with head lineman Ralph
Vaughan, Bouckville, New York, early 1950s.

46   Detail from Asher Brown Durand's High Point:
Shandaken Mountains, 1853. Metropolitan Museum of
Art, New York.

57   No Trespassing sign denoting City of New York Water
Supply property.

72   Steve and Agnes Miller, photographed in Union Grove,
New York, January 24, 1942.

73   Bob Kabat and Sandy (newly Sandy, no longer Lois)
Elmore at Oberlin College; photograph undated.

101   My mom and me on a dirt road in Vermont.

135   Typed business letters included notations for the typist because often the sender—a man—didn't type or wouldn't type, and his secretary (or, here, his wife) would. The sender's initials would be in all caps, separated by a colon from the typist's initials in lowercase.

142   Harvey Hubbell's Calico Indian disguise. Photograph by David Rainbird; disguise from the Hubbell family collection.

144   Detail from an Anti-Rent poster for a Fourth of July protest in Rensselaer County, New York, where the Anti-Rent uprising began.

153   *Down-Rent War, Around 1845* by Mary Earley, 1940, Delhi Post Office, Delhi, New York.

169   Jay Gould and Hamilton Burhans, circa 1855.

182   Harvey Hubbell; photograph undated. Used with permission of the Hubbell family.

192   Papa and Mom Elmore (Granville Sandusky Elmore and Jemima Tennessee Poplin); photograph undated.

199   Portrait of Osman N. Steele. Two copies exist: one in the Andes Society for History and Culture, the other in the county courthouse. One of the portraits was likely made after Steele's death, given how newsworthy his murder was. The original painting was probably made by an itinerant portrait painter, using a stock pose. The details of Steele's face would have been inserted, and the hands are out of proportion with his body. Used with permission of the Andes Society for History and Culture. Photograph by David Rainbird.

223   William Brisbane, 1886, age 74.

230   My parents in Upstate New York, where they worked together on a co-op, sharing life, dreams, and collective values.

Additional Resources

Henry Christman, *Tin Horns and Calico: A Decisive Episode in the Emergence of Democracy*, Bicentennial Edition [as in US Bicentennial] (Cornwallville, NY: Hope Farm Press, 1978). Originally published in 1945 by Henry Holt.

Reeve Huston, *Land and Freedom: Rural Society, Popular Protest, and Party Politics in Antebellum New York* (New York: Oxford University Press, 2000).

Dorothy Kubik, *A Free Soil—A Free People: The Anti-Rent War in Delaware County, New York* (Fleischmanns, NY: Purple Mountain Press, 1997).

Mark A. Lause, *Young America: Land, Labor, and the Republican Community* (Urbana: University of Illinois Press, 2005).

Albert Champlin Mayham, *The Anti-Rent War On Blenheim Hill, An Episode Of The 40's: A History Of The Struggle Between Landlord And Tenant* (Jefferson, NY: Frederick L. Frazee, 1906).

John D. Monroe, *The Anti-Rent War in Delaware County New York: The Revolt against the Rent System* (printed by the author, copy 41 of 100 copies, 1940).

John D. Monroe, *Chapters in the History of Delaware County* (Delhi, NY: Delaware County Historical Association, 1949).

Permission Credits

Noam Chomsky quoted with permission from the International Workers of the World. I want to thank them, too, for the ongoing, century-long commitment to worker solidarity and one big union.

Undersheriff Craig DuMond quoted thanks to Lissa Harris and the *Watershed Post*.

Ian Parks, "Goldenrod," *Shell Island* (Oxfordshire: Waywiser Press, 2006) quoted with the author's permission.

Some lines in the book have been previously published in 4Columns and the Weeklings, and this book would have been impossible without the support of *Granta*, who published "Ghostlands," my initial essay exploring the Anti-Rent War, in 2019.

Acknowledgments

I write from Munsee-Lenape land, much of which was never ceded, and this book is borne of thinking about the multiple meanings of this place. All the errors are mine.

Writing can be isolating but is not singular. None of this would have been possible without the great generosity of multiple communities. Deep and heartfelt thanks to the friends who have been with me in this project from the very start: Diana Evans, Rudd Hubbell, Chris Kraus, Laura Marris, Anna Moschovakis, and Luke Neima. For their support, conversations, and insight: Paul Chaat Smith, Iris Cushing, Adrian Shirk, Lynne Tillman, Jenny Monick, Ian Parks, Jennifer Krasinski, Dan Fox, Steve and Jane Miller, Mike and Becky Porter, the Taylor family, Burr Hubbell, Barb Hubbell, the Margaretville Fire Department (serving with you is my greatest honor), Robert Bruce Mateer, Gary Rosa, Dick Sanford, David Godwin, Jennifer Higgie, Roz Foster, Claire Boyle, Jonathan Lethem, Ania Szremski, Colleen Asper, Jessica Lynne, Jody Kahn, Corinna Ripps Schaming, Ellie Ga, Bronwyn Keenan, Marlene McCarty, Jodi Lynn Maracle, Pareesa Pourian, Kate Newby, Mina Takahashi, Alina Bliumis, John Mollett, Ira Silverberg, Lissa Harris, Shirley Sanford, Georgie Smith, Clint Balcom, as well as the School of Visual Arts's Design Criticism MA and now-defunct Art Writing MFA. My gratitude to so many historians: Diane Galusha, the Delaware County Historical Association: Ray Lafever, Tim Duerden, and Angela Gaffney; the Andes Society for History and Culture: Joanne Kosuda-Warner and Linda Dunne; Laurence M. Hauptman, the Delaware County Clerk's Office.

Thank you, Halley Parry and Jaclyn Gilbert. I am still dazzled by Joey McGarvey and Daniel Slager's sharing my vision for twinned books tied to my small town, exploring time and socialism. I appreciate their editorial care and collaboration. Thank you to the generosity of everyone at Milkweed Editions: Lauren Langston Klein, Mary Austin Speaker, Yanna Demkiewicz, and Morgan LaRocca. Working with you has been singularly rewarding. I am also grateful to Erika Stevens who has been attentive to the ideas here from their very inception.

Thank you to my family, my sisters Ellen Kabat and Gale Kabat, who have walked in woods and over hills and mountains with me; and to David Rainbird for everything— for reading, for listening, for leaving your homeland, for wandering across field and forest together.

Having Joan Nelson's "Untitled, 2021" on the cover is thrilling. I've long wanted to write about her work. Her paintings are mesmerizing dreamscapes as a response to this landscape where she and I both live. She renders it psychedelic and strange, and her work stands as a question (or comeback) to the often male and overwhelmingly white American landscape tradition that grew out of these mountains. Instead of oil paint in glazes, she layers up spray paint and glitter and sometimes glitter spray paint. In her compositions there's also mascara and nail polish, even hair filler fibers. The surfaces change at different times of the day, or as you change and as you walk by, as if you and I—we together—are part of the painting and its process.

Crucial support was provided in the pandemic from the NYFA Keep NYS Creating Project Grant.

JENNIFER KABAT received an Andy Warhol Foundation Arts Writers Grant for her criticism and has been published in *BOMB* and *The Best American Essays*. Her writing has also appeared in *Granta, Frieze, Harper's, McSweeney's, The Believer, Virginia Quarterly Review, Los Angeles Review of Books, The New York Review,* and *The White Review*. A finalist for the essay prize at Notting Hill Editions, she often collaborates with artists. She's part of the core faculty in the Design Research MA at the School of Visual Arts. An apprentice herbalist, she lives in rural Upstate New York and serves on her volunteer fire department.

milkweed
EDITIONS

Founded as a nonprofit organization in 1980, Milkweed
Editions is an independent publisher. Our mission is to
identify, nurture, and publish transformative literature,
and build an engaged community around it.

Milkweed Editions is based in Bdé Óta Othúŋwe
(Minneapolis) within Mní Sota Makhóčhe, the
traditional homeland of the Dakhóta people. Residing
here since time immemorial, Dakhóta people still
call Mní Sota Makhóčhe home, with four federally
recognized Dakhóta nations and many more Dakhóta
people residing in what is now the state of Minnesota.
Due to continued legacies of colonization, genocide,
and forced removal, generations of Dakhóta people
remain disenfranchised from their traditional homeland.
Presently, Mní Sota Makhóčhe has become a refuge and
home for many Indigenous nations and peoples, including
seven federally recognized Ojibwe nations.
We humbly encourage our readers to reflect upon the
historical legacies held in the lands they occupy.

milkweed.org

Milkweed Editions, an independent nonprofit literary publisher, gratefully acknowledges sustaining support from our board of directors, the McKnight Foundation, the National Endowment for the Arts, and many generous contributions from foundations, corporations, and thousands of individuals—our readers. This activity is made possible by the voters of Minnesota through a Minnesota State Arts Board Operating Support grant, thanks to a legislative appropriation from the arts and cultural heritage fund.

Interior design by Mary Austin Speaker
Typeset in Adobe Jenson Pro

Adobe Jenson was designed by Robert Slimbach for
Adobe and released in 1996. Slimbach based Jenson's
roman styles on a text face cut by fifteenth-century type
designer Nicolas Jenson, and its italics are based on type
created by Ludovico Vicentino degli Arrighi,
a late fifteenth-century papal scribe
and type designer.